The Romance of Scholar's Stones

頑石山房藏石心路

The ROMANCE *of* SCHOLARS' STONES

Adventures in Appreciation

Kemin Hu

Floating World Editions

First edition, 2011

ISBN: 978-1-891640-61-2
Library of Congress Cataloging-in-Publication data available

p. ii shows *Xian Ren Feng (Immortal Peak)*
Lingbi stone, Lingbi County, Anhui province
48 x 26 x16 cm, 16th c or earlier burl wood stand

p. iii shows *Scholar with Scholars' Rock*
Carved stone with porcelain figure
40 x 20 x 11 cm, 20th c carved stone stand

Colophon page shows: *Xiao ZhouYun (Little Wrinkled Cloud)*
Yellow Wax Stone, Guangdong province
34 x 15 x 10 cm, 20th c wooden stand

Contents

Preface

Over the more than two decades I have been collecting Chinese scholars' stones, I have experienced many moments of astonishment, as well as some regrets. I look back on my years of collecting as not only a joyful life pursuit but also a constant learning process. Although what I have said in previous books holds true, there are many aspects of stone connoisseurship that if writing those volumes today I would want to elaborate on, based on the experience of my additional years of collecting. As well, I have encountered many questions in researching stone lore. While I do not claim to have answered them all, what I have discovered should be of interest to all collectors of Chinese scholars' rocks.

This book is a collection of seven illustrated essays on various topics related to stone collecting. The first, "Stone Aesthetics in Ancient China," expands on what I have written previously on the four standards of stone appreciation put forward by the Song dynasty scholar Mi Fu, namely, *shou*, *zhou*, *lou*, and *tou*.

Ao Shi Qun Xiong (Leader of All Heroes)
Boshan Wen stone, Shandong province
54 x 32 x 22 cm, 16th c or earlier stone stand

The second chapter looks at *yanshan*, or "Ink Mountain Stones," which, initially having the utilitarian function of making ink, may be the earliest and most widely collected of all stone forms. "In Search of Qingzhou Stones" presents evidence of these as one of the earliest highly valued stone types, and that what constitutes the short list of "best" stones may have changed over time. The essay of appreciation "Nine Wonderful Stones" allows readers to enjoy a diverse sampling of stones acknowledged to be outstanding examples of traditional stone aesthetics. Though most of these ancient stones do not have inscriptions or written records about them, we can still glean much about their origins and history from their shapes and patinas, as well as from the material, quality, and style of their bases.

"A Treasure from the Han Dynasty" deserves a more detailed introduction. In 2007 I was fortunate enough to acquire the *Kunming Stone*, the focus of the chapter. This acquisition aroused in me a deep interest in the ancient records associated with it; according to the *Genealogy of the Li Family*, this wonderful object has been kept in their family for nearly 250 years. Moreover, since the Song dynasty noted

San Feng (Triple Peaks)
Lingbi stone *yanshan*, Lingbi county, Anhui province
36 x 30 x 18 cm, 18th to 19th c wooden stand

Opposite: *Bie You Dong Tian (Cave Leading to a Heavenly Realm)*
Calico Lingbi stone, Lingbi county, Anhui province
50 x 36 x 14 cm, 19th c Jiangnan style wooden stand

scholars had composed poems and testimonials in praise of this stone, recorded in this reliable chronicle that claims the stone had been passed down from the time of Emperor Wu of the Western Han dynasty. Although much needs to be confirmed, and may never be, the research undertaken to seek confirmation has been as rigorous and systematic as writing an academic paper, giving me a more profound understanding of the history and culture of the Han.

In the course of my researches I have translated a number of ancient Chinese texts on stone appreciation, some of which I present in "Selected Ancient Writings on Stones." Finally, we look at a gallery of stone-related objects, including stone-like forms fashioned from a variety of materials. Together with the previous essays and appreciations, and especially with the interesting mystery of the *Kunming Stone*, these offer powerful material proof for stone worship and appreciation in ancient China.

I am greatly indebted to Sun Zhaojun, Yu Ying, and Zhao Gang, and Ray Furse for their help. Thanks also to my family and all those who share my interest in stones and have assisted me over my many years of researching and collecting them.

Stone Aesthetics in Ancient China

The criteria used for evaluating stones in ancient China were unique, and remain very important in the appreciation and collection of scholars' rocks today. Though I have referred to the "four judging criteria" in previous books, especially my *Scholars' Rocks in Ancient China: The Suyuan Stone Catalogue* (hereafter *Scholars' Rocks*), I did not present them in any detail, which I hope to do in this essay.

From ancient times, men of letters discussed various ways to determine and describe the value of the stones they collected. The most obvious distinction was by stone type, which was closely related to the stone's source. Bai Juyi (772–846), a renowned poet of the Tang dynasty, ranked stones from the lake Taihu as the very best, and as second best those from Luofu and Tianzhu (mountains in Guangdong and Zhejiang provinces, respectively). In his essay "Notes on Taihu Stones," Bai relates how then Prime Minister Niu Seng-ru (779–847) regarded stones as "guests and friends" and as "sages and men of virtue, treasuring them like precious jades and loving them like his own children." Niu assigned each stone to one of four major classes, each of which had three sub-classes. The later emergence of Lingbi and Ying stones changed this ranking. As stated in the section "Stone Judging Criteria" of the *Zhang Wu Zhi* (written from 1621 to 1627, and translated as *On Superfluous Things*), an important work by Wen Zhenheng (1585–1624) of the Ming Dynasty (1368–1644): "When it comes to stones, Lingbi stones are the best and Ying stones the second best. Both are scarce, and expensive for collectors."

Pian Pian Qi Wu (Lightly Dancing Couple)
Boshan Wen stone, Shandong province
74 x 44 x 17 cm, 18th to 19th c wooden stand

The four judging criteria most often referred to by stone collectors was put forward by Mi Fu (1051–1107), well-known literatus of the Song dynasty (960–1279). According to him, four characteristics, namely *shou*, *zhou*, *lou*, and *tou* should be considered when appreciating or evaluating stones. Combining sensory perception and rational analysis, this methodology has been accepted by stone lovers from the Song dynasty and is still in use today.

The Song dynasty Mi Fu lived in was a flourishing period for China's stone collectors. Many men of letters collected them, and even the Song emperors were noted stone lovers. These elites aspired to a

Qi Feng Tian Zhu (Grotesque Peak Like a Heavenly Pillar)
Lingbi stone, Lingbi county, Anhui province
125 x 24 x 18 cm, 20th c tree root stand

simple life of naturalness, spontaneity, and creativity, influenced by the Daoist doctrine of *wuwei*. Literally meaning "without action," *wuwei* is best interpreted not as doing nothing but rather acting spontaneously, in accordance with one's nature. A tree for example, was not seen as "trying to grow," it simply grew because it was natural to do so. Likewise, Song literati attempted to incorporate this quality in both their lives and their aesthetic judgments.

As a member of this group, Mi Fu was well versed in the arts of calligraphy, painting, and poetry, and for this reason was once summoned by the Emperor Huizong (1082–1135) of the Northern Song dynasty to serve in the Academy of Calligraphy and Painting. Mi Fu was noted for his elegant but unconstrained cursive script, which flows with vigor yet follows strictly the rules of calligraphy. He did not yield to what was in vogue in painting, but was continually bent on innovation. *Cloudy Mountains*, a painting by Mi Fu's son Mi Youren (1074–1151) is considered reflective of his father's style and influence. It has been held in high esteem by Chinese art lovers due to its use of large wet dots of ink (called "Mi-family dots") applied with a flat brush to depict the mountains and villages

Shen Nu Feng (Goddess Peak)
Lingbi stone, Lingbi county, Anhui province
28 x 15 x 15 cm, 19th to 20th c wooden stand

shrouded in mist, a natural scene typical of parts of southern China. Unconventional and uninhibited in behavior, Mi Fu was even widely known as Madman Mi because he once declared an impressive stone to be his own brother and bowed to it in a display of the deference given to family elders.

Mi Fu's four judging criteria for stone appreciation shows his profound aesthetic cultivation and his fine connoisseurship, both developed over time through personal experience. Holding offices in different places, Mi had the opportunity to see and to admire almost all famous stones and highly regarded stone types, including Lingbi, Ying, and Taihu stones. He had a rich collection of stones and we could say was obsessed with them. As is recorded in a section "Cangxue Hall Mountain Inkstone" of the *Suyuan* catalogue, Mi Fu once held office in Lianshui, a place adjacent to Lingbi, and therefore had many fine examples of those stones. He would appreciate them individually and give each an appropriately impressive name. It was written that when he entered the studio in where his collection was stored, "he would stay there the whole day." Mi Fu's criteria for aesthetic evaluation were based on four qualities, as follows.

Feng Huang Zhan Chi (Phoenix Soaring to Great Heights)
Yingwo Wen stone
21 x 32 x 17 cm, 19th c wooden stand

Shou

Shou (literally, "thin" or "lean") is the quality of appearing slim and elegant. Such stones typically stand tall and straight, with firm peaks, overall appearing imposing and resolute (opposite). *Shou* also means that a stone must be graceful, not cumbersome, although some stones that are not slim or tall may still have this quality (above). As well, although most stones exhibiting powerful *shou* may appear imposing due to their height and robust peaks, others may look more charming and even delicate due to their slim elegance. All the four stone types most lauded from ancient times have examples meeting the highest standard of *shou*. A Ying stone named *Old Man Rock*, from the collection of Richard Rosenblum's family and now in the Museum of Fine Arts, Boston, is considered a particularly fine example of *shou*.

Right: *Ming Lu Feng (Deer Cry Peak)*
Boshan Wen stone, Shandong province
117 x 25 x 14 cm, 19th c northern style wooden stand

Liang Jian Feng (Sword Peak)
Stone type unknown
46 x 11 x 11 cm, 19th to 20th c wooden stand

Chi Feng Dou Bi (Steep Red Cliff)
Stone type unknown
49 x 24 x 15 cm, 17th to 18th c tree root stand

Below: *ZhouYun Feng (Wrinkled Cloud Peak)*
Ying stone, Yingde county, Guangdong province
h 260 cm, Jiangnan Famous Stone Garden, Hangzhou

ZhuangYuan Shi (Foremost Scholar Stone)
Ying stone, Yingde county, Guangdong province
63 x 24 x 12 cm, 19th to 20th c wooden stand

Zhou

Zhou (literally, "wrinkles" or "creases") refers to the ancient and intriguing crisscrossed grooves of a stone's surface, which may be reflected in the overall stone shape, to resemble either towering ridges and peaks or range upon range of mountains. For purposes of discussing stone aesthetics, the surface wrinkles can be thought of as "small *zhou*" and the creased stone shape considered "big *zhou*." The wrinkles vary in form for different stone types, for example, those on Lingbi stones have sesame or walnut look, or appear like the wrinkles of dried dates, while those on Boshan Wen stones are like intertwining dots and dashes, imparting an intriguing beauty. The characteristics of *zhou* are often best seen in Ying stones, a traditional stone type (right). Ying stones found in Guangdong and Guangxi have rich texture and are typically craggy and wrinkled on the surface, with smooth, deep pits. The curving shapes, on the other hand, can better exhibit the miraculous natural wonders of an ever-changing universe. *Wrinkled Cloud Peak*, a tall, garden Ying stone located in Hangzhou (opposite), is generally considered among the finest examples of *zhou*.

Left: *Bai Zhou Yun (White Wrinkled Cloud)*
White Ying stone
48 x 26 x 16 cm, 17th to 18th c Shanxi style wooden stand

Shen Long Feng (Magical Dragon Peak)
Lingbi stone, Lingbi county, Anhui province
82 x 42 x 24 cm, 19th c tree root stand

Xiang Long Shi (Auspicious Dragon Stone)
Ying stone, Yingde county, Guangdong province
28 x 21 x 16 cm, 18th c *huanghuali* wooden stand

Ceng Yun Feng (Thousand Layered Cloud)
Lingbi stone, Lingbi county, Anhui province
22 x 23 x 14 cm, 18th c wooden stand

Left: *Du Xiu Feng (Distinctive Mountain Peak)*
Ying stone, Yingde county, Guangdong province
40 x 14 x 10 cm, 19th to 20th c wooden stand

Jin Shan ShenYue (Essence of Golden Mountain Peak)
Stone type unknown
49 x 24 x 25 cm, 17th to 18th c wooden stand

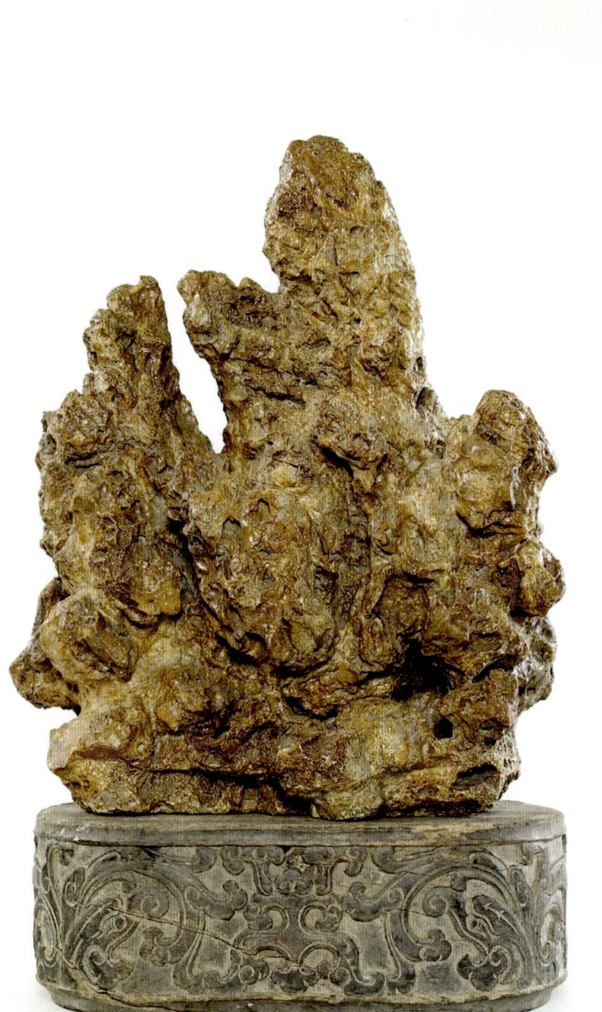

Left: *Xi Yun Feng (Joyful Peak)*
Ying stone, Yingde county, Guangdong province
19 x 10 x 6 cm, 19th c wooden stand

Qiucui Shi (Mount Qiucui Stone)
Stone type unknown
34 x 32 x 18 cm, 20th c wooden stand

Left: *Chun Feng Song Wo Shang Qin Tian*
(Transported to Heaven by a Spring Breeze)
Ying stone, Yingde county, Guangdong province
52 x 30 x 18 cm, 20th c tree root stand

Bing Jing Feng (Ice Crystal Peak)
Xuan stone, Anhui province
39 x 16 x 13 cm, 18th to 19th c southern syle wooden stand

Opposite: *Wu Yun Feng (Dancing Cloud Summit)*
Lingbi stone, Lingbi county, Anhui province
39 x 19 x 12 cm, 17th to 18th c wooden stand

Above: *JinYun Ping (Brocade Cloud Screen)*
Yellow wax stone, Guangdong province
28 x 28 x 8 cm, 19th c open southern style wooden stand

Han ZhuYu (Pearl Harboring Jade)
Yellow wax stone, Guangdong province
11 x 12 x 6 cm, 19th c open southern style wooden stand

Hu Ji (Infinity)
Kun stone, Kunshan county, Jiangsu province
31 x 21 x 10 cm, 19th c open southern style wooden stand

Lou

Lou (literally, "to leak" or "to drip," as from holes) in the case of stones refers to the interconnected channels or other joined interior interstices. Sometimes they are linked to one another with great intricacy, as if three-dimensional passageways were meandering throughout the rock (left). *Lou* is not a common quality of scholar's rocks, but it is highly prized and one that can best distinguish natural from man-made examples. Though artistic embellishment is possible on the surface of an artwork, it is much difficult, if not impossible, to execute on the inside. However, the erosive power of natural elements like water, air, and sand can and do, over thousands of years, "process" stones from inside, producing holes, openings, and interconnected channels within. Very few stones exhibit the highest standard of *lou*, most often Taihu stones, whose channels are the result of long-term water erosion. *Yu Ling Long*, a large, garden Taihu stone found in Shanghai, is said to fully exhibit the characteristics of *lou*. When water drips down from one of the upper holes, it will flow out of the other holes, including those near the bottom. When incense

Right: *Xiang Yun Shi (Auspicious Cloud Stone)*
Unknown stone type
65 x 35 x 20 cm, 19th to 20th c wooden stand

Yu Ling Long (Exquisite Jade)
Taihu stone, Jiangsu province
45 x 27 x 25 cm, 20th c rose wood stand

is lit at one of the bottom holes, the fragrant smoke will stream out of the upper holes.

Two stones in Chinese stone history deserve mention here. One is *Baojin Zhai Yanshan* (*Baojin Studio Mountain Inkstone,* see p. 35) once owned by Emperor Li Yu, the scholar Mi Fu, and Emperor Huizhong in succession. According to records, "This stone has an upper hole and a lower hole. Though they seem not linked to each other from outside, water dripping down from the upper hole would flow out of the lower hole after some time. This shows that the two holes are connected by a channel inside." Therefore, those who saw the stone could not help sighing, "There is another world inside, which is really fascinating." The other stone is *Xiao You Dong Tian* (*Little Cave Paradise*, see *Scholars' Rocks,* p. 62) once owned by Su Shi in the Song dynasty. Inside its base was hidden an incense burner. When incense was lit, smoke would stream out of the holes at the top, looking like clouds encircling the peaks. Both stones are excellent examples of *lou*, with networks of channels allowing water and smoke to pass through with ease.

Juan Lang Shi (Sweeping Wave Stone)
Boshan Wen stone, Shandong province
37 x 41 x 19 cm, 18th c northern style wooden stand

Tou

Tou (literally "to pass through," or "to penetrate") means openness, a result of multiple holes, often conveying a feeling of transparency. Some stones have holes within holes, through which light can pass, creating scenes of delicate beauty. Caves (*dong*) were an important concept in Daoism, the indigenous religion of early China; sealed off from the outside except for apertures letting in air and water, they were a metaphor for the inner workings of the body, thus ideal places to hone one's spirituality through meditation. In the popular imagination, they were also considered the abode of Daoist adepts and celestial beings. The stone *Dong Tian Fu Di* (literally, *Cave Heaven, Auspicious Land*, see p. 72) describes an abode of immortals, with *dong* the entrance to that realm. The man-made hills in Chinese classical garden design usually have holes and caves in them, some even with moon-shaped gates marked *Bie You Dong Tian*, meaning "Beyond is the Realm of Immortals," which leads to a heavenly scene within. Though the Daoist connotations of *dong* are important to the imagery of *tou*, the term is broader. *Tou* refers not only to holes, but also to openings that pass clear through, allowing sunlight and moonlight shine through and making a stone come alive. Most traditional stones may exhibit naturally formed caves and holes, with the easily eroded Taihu stones particularly well known for such natural features.

As one might suppose, these standards are both independent and interrelated. *Tou* (holes) are closely related to *lou* (channels), which can be considered extensions of surface holes. As well, both *lou* and *tou* can make a stone appear *shou* (thin). In fact, few ancient stones can fully satisfy the four standards, except for some Taihu stones. What deserves emphasis is that the best stones are not necessarily perfect in all these aspects, and in judging any stone we also should take into account such criteria as quality, color, and sound.

Although for hundreds of years connoisseurs have used Mi Fu's four judging criteria for stone appreciation, no records have been found to verify the exact time and place Mi Fu put forward his standards. The Song Dynasty *Yuyang Stone Catalogue* by Li You Yong (n.d.) records that: "Yuanzhuang [the style name of Mi Fu] mentioned four standards of stone appreciation, namely, *xiu* [elegant], *shou* [thin], *ya* [refined], and *tou*

Two views of *Zhong QiuYue (Full Moon at Autumn Hill)*
Lingbi stone, Lingbi county, Anhui province
71 x 37 x 18 cm, 20th c wooden stand

[with holes], which, inexhaustive as they may be, cover most of the beauty of a stone." Notice that here *zhou* and *lou* are replaced with *xiu* and *ya*. Sometime later this was changed, as indicated in the colophon written for a painting *Stone* by the famed literatus Zheng Banqiao (aka Zheng Xie; 1693–1765). According to Zheng, "The standards of stone appreciation put forward by Mi Yuanzhang, namely, *shou*, *zhou*, *lou*, and *tou* have indeed described all the merits of a fine stone."

It is difficult for us to know whether the author of the *Yuyang Stone Catalogue* made a mistake or stone connoisseurs after Mi Fu modified his original standards, but it is not important. The four criteria, it can be said, are based on Mi Fu's own experience and his understanding of comments on stones made by his predecessors, with the testing and modification of later stone collectors. Perhaps because *xiu* and *ya* are more subjective judgments that could vary greatly among viewers, while *zhou* and *lou* are more objective, and so less likely to vary, stone collectors over time have come to favor the latter.

In any case, with the emergence of new stone types in China, the colorful and geometric Red River stone for example (p. 26), Mi Fu's standards are no longer able to describe all stone qualities. For this reason a new set of standards has become current in China: an evaluation of shape, material, color, and grain. In fact, the old criteria do not contradict the new, for different stone types may require different standards. The old standards are mainly used to judge traditional stone types and focus particularly on shape, while the new criteria appear unique among other standard of artistic judgment. The new standard can be further modified into "shape, material, color, and spirit," the latter consideration very appropriate for stone judgment. While it is true that shape is the most fundamental quality of a fine stone—for without shape there would be no spirit to speak of—still, a finely shaped stone lacking in spirit can hardly be considered exceptional. For example, one stone may look like the very model of a fish while another may not look explicitly like a fish at first sight, but conveys the impression of a fish energetically leaping from a stream. The latter we would consider the better stone, and this is why we must take spirit into consideration when judging. What is called "grain" in

QingYun Shi (Celebrating Clouds Stone)
Lingbi stone, Lingbi county, Anhui province
48 x 40 x 22 cm, 17th to 18th c northern style wooden stand

Shu Feng Lou Yue (Flowing Moonlight and Breezes)
Taihu stone, Jiangsu province
57 x 39 x 20 cm, 18th to 19th c northern style wooden stand

Da Qiu Ru Zhuo (Homely Appearance Concealing Great Wisdom)
Stone type unknown
28 x 15 x 15 cm, 17th to 18th c wooden stand

Below: *BiYu TianYan (Green Jade with Sky Eye)*
Red River stone, Tahua county, Guangxi province
30 x 28 x 15 cm, 20th c wooden stand

the revised criteria is in fact an element of shape or, to be more exact, resembles *zhou* in the old criteria and thus can be replaced by "spirit."

From the earliest recorded Chinese philosophy and legend, stones have been considered the "bones of the earth." As a product of nature, they often resembled shapes from nature, not only mountains and peaks, but also birds, fish, waves, etc., Although admired for that quality, such similarities were more often abstract than representational, not exact likenesses so much as a resemblance in spirit. In fact, this latter quality may be considered the most important of all when judging stones. Even though a stone is essentially an oddly shaped, inanimate object, so long as it has spirit, it can convey the vigor and majesty of nature, striking a responsive chord in the hearts of the viewers. Hence, a stone with great spirit will be judged among the finest, and this is surely what caused Mi Fu to bow.

Fei Fei Shi (No No Stone)
Lingbi stone, Lingbi county, Anhui province
32 x 39 x 9 cm, 19th to 20th c wooden stand

Opposite: *Song Zi Guanyin (Boy-Bestowing Guanyin)*
Lingbi stone, Lingbi county, Anhui province
45 x 25 x 12 cm, 18th c wooden stand

Right: *Yu Gu Pan (Amorous Glance)*
Taihu stone, Jiangsu province
60 x 30 x 12 cm, 18th to 19th c wooden stand

Below: *Yuan Shi (Destiny Stone)*
Lingbi stone, Lingbi county, Anhui province
15 x 22 x 9 cm, with two inscriptions, 20th c wooden stand

Inscription by modern *penjing* master Dong Shuyu reads: "This stone with moist color and clear sound can viewed from eight directions. It came from a rock left by the goddess Nuwa when she patched the sky. I obtained it at Lengtan in the spring of 1963. It was once a treasure of Emperor Huizhong in the Xuanhe period [1119–25] of the Northern Song dynasty. I wrote this to record my joy in acquiring it."

Fei Feng Tan Yue (Soaring to Clouds Pinnacle)
Lingbi stone *yanshan*, Lingbi county, Anhui province
34 x 32 x 12 cm, 18th to 19th c Jiangnan style wooden stand

The Earliest Collected Stone Form

Three emperors in Chinese history are considered exceptional for their literary and artistic talents: Li Yu (937–978) of the Southern Tang dynasty; Huizong (1082–1135) of the Northern Song dynasty; and Qianlong (1711–1799) of the Qing dynasty. All had a passion for stone collecting, in particular a type called *yanshan*, literally "ink mountain," essentially a mountain shaped stone with a depression or well for grinding and mixing ink. I noted in my *Scholars' Rocks in Ancient China* (p. 75) that the first documented creator of *yanshan* was Li Yu, a noted connoisseur and an emperor well versed in poetry, calligraphy, and painting. However, practical use of the *yanshan* form must extend much further back in Chinese history, as evidenced by ceramic models (p.32) from the Han dynasty (206 BCE–220 CE).

The increased popularity of *yanshan* in the Southern Tang resulted from Li Yu's unsparing effort to acquire fine examples of the "four treasures of the study" (*wenfang sibao*), namely, brush, inkstick, paper, and inkstone, the latter used to grind the inkstick with water to produce ink. The *Baojin Studio Yanshan* and *Cangxue Studio Yanshan*, two masterpieces of Chinese stone art (p. 35, upper left and right respectively), were first created by Emperor Li Yu, later to be acquired by Mi Fu and Emperor Huizong in succession. The *Baojin Studio Yanshan* has now been passed down through succeeding generations for about 700 years. No wonder the eighteenth-century collector Lu Xuan was moved to say upon seeing it (as recorded in Hu Pu-an's *Qishi Ji*, or *Record of Strange Stones*): "Where are the rivers and mountains of the [Southern] Tang Dynasty? They can be seen today only in a stone such as this!"

Apart from Li Yu, the emperors Huizong and Qianlong were also avid connoisseurs of *yanshan*. The former's passion for stones is well documented. According to the *Tiewei Shan Congtan* (*Collection of Talks from Iron Mountain*) by Cai Tao of the Song Dynasty, Huizong had collected a number of *yanshan* for his palace and created another two himself. Those Huizong collected are also mentioned several times in the *Suyuan Shipu (Plain Garden Stone Catalogue)* by Lin Youlin of the Ming dynasty, many passages of which are translated in my *Scholar's Rocks in Ancient China*. In the section about Lingbi stones (*Scholars' Rocks*, p. 35), Lin relates that Xiang Zijing, a famous

Inkslab with Twelve Peaks
Ceramic, Han Dynasty (206 BCE–220 CE)
7 x 20 cm, Palace Museum, Beijing

collector in the Ming dynasty, had a Lingbi stone once owned by Emperor Huizong, on the back of which was inscribed that it entered Huizong's collection in March of the first year of the Xuanhe period (1082).

The interest in *yanshan* appears to have propelled the burgeoning popularity of collecting of scholars' rocks in Song China. It is probably due to its relation to the "four treasures" that *yanshan* came to be the most typical form of scholar's rocks. *Yanshan* in the Tang and Song normally had ink basins, and therefore retained their functional quality. Since the ink basins resembled lakes and ponds, these objects embodied twin values of natural beauty and practicality, even though most of the basins were not natural but carved. However *yanshan* also came to be appreciated as much for their portrayal of topography as for their function. And since two of the stone types most noted for their evocation of distant mountain ridges and peaks, namely Lingbi and Ying, were much harder to carve, they often lacked basins. Therefore, during the Ming and Qing dynasties, ink basins became a less critical component of *yanshan*, and evaluation came to be focused on their aesthetic qualities alone.

Deeply influenced by Daoism, men of letters in ancient China revered nature and were passionate about rivers and mountains, subjects that permeate Chinese painting and poetry. They valued the ability of *yanshan* to conjure in miniature landscapes through which they could commune with nature and even embark on virtual journeys without leaving their studios. According to them, "[viewing] mountain shapes condenses in the moment a scene that extends thousands of miles. Through a small stone one can experience the immenseness and wonder of nature." Not simply observing *yanshan*, but rather actually communing with their stones, enhanced their aesthetic sensitivities and inspired deeper insights, which were developed through their painting and poetry. Following are some poems and comments on *yanshan* written by scholar-collectors:

> The mountain is high,
> the moon small;
> the stone reveals as the water ebbs.
>
> —"Yutou Stone," by Emperor Song Huizong

Animal-shaped Water Dispenser
Jade, Song dynasty (960–1279)
14 x 6.6 cm, Capital Museum, Beijing

"Why should one take the trouble to visit noted mountains? Here in his palm he can appreciate the ridges and peaks."

—"Comments on a Luofu Stone," by Li Deyu of the Tang dynasty

"The twelve peaks emerging amid clouds and rains, this *yanshan* boasts the endowment of nature's art."

—"Yuntao Stone," by Huang Tingjian of the Song Dynasty

"There emerge hundreds of cliffs and thousands of valleys, with a steep gully connected in the middle by a river in the sky."

—"Xiao Dai Yue," by Zhao Ziang of the Yuan dynasty

"I feel astonished viewing this stone from afar. Elegant and graceful, it appears unique and extraordinary; I cannot remember where I became acquainted with it; but the gullies and valleys remind me of Mount Wuyi."

—"Comments on a Stone," by Pu Songling of the Qing dynasty

Mi Fu's Yanshan

As mentioned earlier, the six-peak *Baojin Studio Yanshan* and thirty-six-peak *Cangxue Studio Yanshan* (also known as *Haiyue'an Yanshan*), were both owned by Emperor Li Yu and later by Mi Fu. Mi Fu subsequently exchanged the former stone with his friend Xue Shaopeng (styled Daozu) and traded the latter to Su Zhongrong for a fine garden house, an indication of its value. But he later came to regret profoundly both exchanges and when he went to visit Xue to enjoy his former possession, he was refused. His feelings after parting with the stone are vividly recalled in one of his poems:

I am no longer able to see the stone,
All I can do is write poems and sigh.
There is only the jade toad
To shed tears with me.

The "jade toad" is a water container, also now sadly alone without the inkstone it would have supplied.

During the following six centuries, the stone changed owners many times. It was once in the

Yanshan Ming (Epigram on an Ink Mountain Stone)
Calligraphy by Mi Fu (1051–1107)
Palace Museum, Beijing

possession of Zhu Yizun (1629–1709), a literary man of the Qing dynasty, in whose family it was passed down as a treasure for four generations. His friend Wang Shizhen (1674–1711) wrote two poems for this *yanshan* after seeing it at the Zhu's home. One states:

> This precious *yanshan* of the Southern Tang
> has suffered many disasters.
> Now it accompanies a hermit writing books,
> Its elegant ridges and peaks intact.
> There is no need to shed tears with the jade toad.

Mi Fu also composed an epigram (above) in praise of another *yanshan* he once possessed:

> The ink under light shows five colors and the mountains around are reflected in it, looking like floating peaks of Kunlun; the ink basin at the top resembles dark clouds, with white veins on the rock like lightning; when the ink flows downward, it appears like a dragon hanging from heaven above Dongting lake, nurturing the land.

Both the Kunlun mountains and Dongting lake figure prominently in Chinese mythology and are abodes of Daoist immortals. From these rich allusions we can imagine the splendor of the stone and understand how much Mi Fu admired it. In 2002, the original epigram (above), which had been found in Japan, appeared at an auction in Beijing and was sold for a record-breaking $3.7 million dollars. It was this auction that heightened the interest of many in researching *yanshan*. Currently, the epigram is kept in the Palace Museum in Beijing.

From historical records, we also know that Mi Fu was not only the owner of the aforementioned well-known *yanshan*, but also of a unique bright-green tiered stone that he describes in "A History of Inkstones":

> I collected a fresh-green piled stone. It is solid and resonant, consisting of three tiers and an ink basin embedded on one side. On the top is a peak, which is more than one *chi* [0.33m] in height and covered by rocks that spread to all sides like clouds. When water is poured down

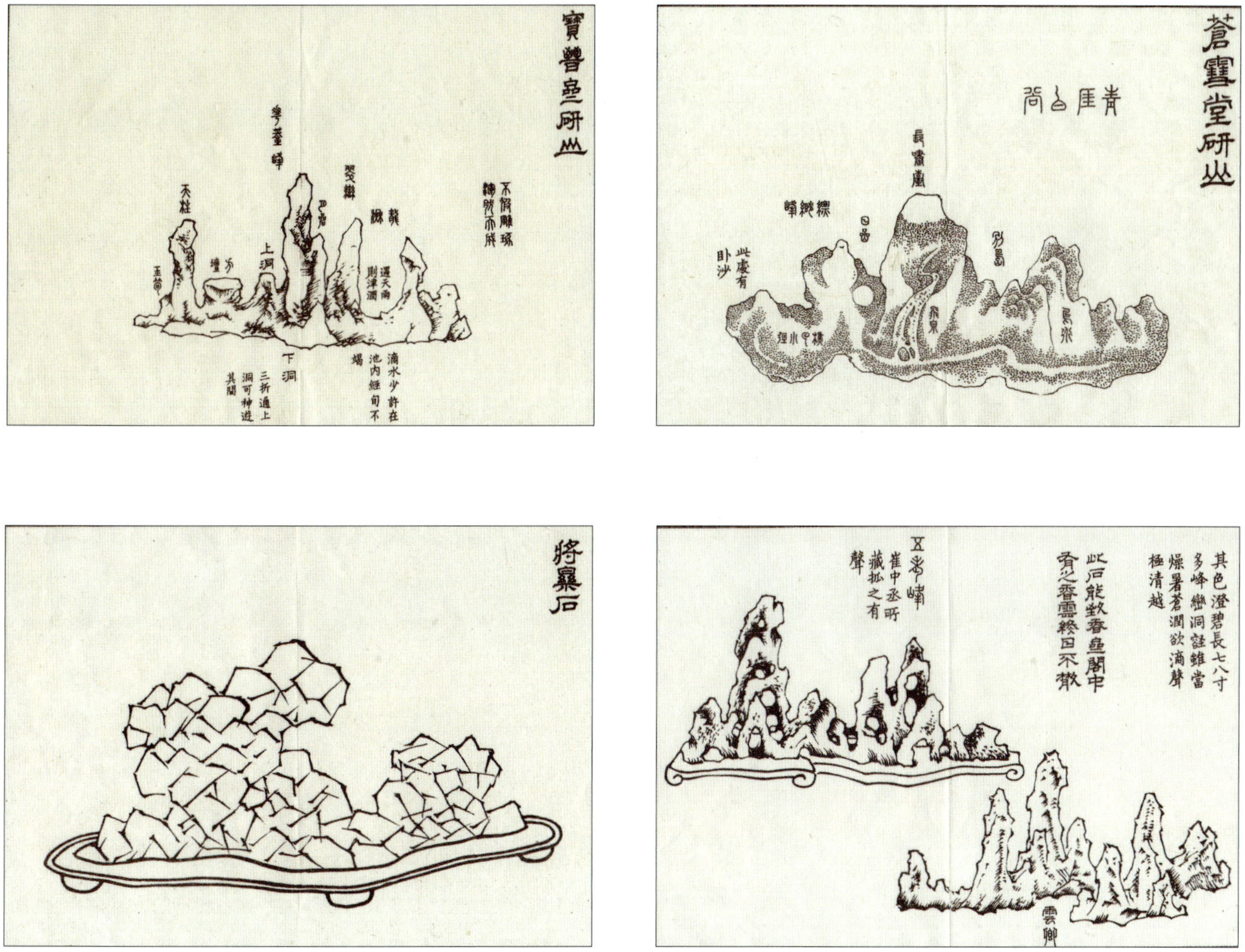

Paintings of *yanshan*, including *Baojin Studio Yanshan* (upper left) and *Cangxue Studio Yanshan* (upper right) from a modern reprint of *Suyuan Shipu (Plain Garden Stone Catalogue)* by Lin Youlin (1578–1647), first printed 1603

Left: *Yanshan Ren (Lover of Yanshan)*
Kun stone, Kunshan city, Jiangsu province
39 x 24 x 10 cm, 18th to 19th c wooden stand
Right: Inscription *"Yanshan Ren"* at peak of stone

> from the top, it will flow down along both sides to the middle of the ink basin. There is an epigram on the stone: "This *yanshan* has been treasured in different times and dynasties."

In his essay "To Qian Mu," Su Shi (1037–1101) wrote of another Mi Fu inkstone: "The day before yesterday I composed an epigram for a *yanshan* of Mi Yuanzhang. The stone is indeed miraculous and was obtained from Mount Shizhongshan in Hukou."

In his preface to the *Yuyang Stone Catalogue*, Li Yu Yang describes another Mi Fu inkstone called *Xiling* (*Joyful Mountain*): "Mi Fu possesses a *yanshan* known as *Xiling*, and on the top of the stone is a heavenly pond with water enough to dip in a writing brush. It is really a miraculous gift of nature."

Volume nine of the Song dynasty *Commentary on Inkstones* by Gao Sisun claims that Mi Fu had a *yanshan* named *Yun Xiu Qi Feng* (*Distant Ranges and Strange Peaks*), which was 17 cm high, 23 cm wide, and 4 cm deep. The stone had two natural peaks, like a host and the guest bowing to each other. At the bottom of the right peak was a flat depression, used as the ink basin. Carved on the stone are not only the four characters *Yun Xiu Qi Feng*, but also *tianran* (natural), *kequan* (lovely spring), and *Zi'ang cang* (collected by Zi'ang). Mention has been made of this *yanshan* in the great eighteenth-century catalogues *Imperially Endorsed Collections of the Four Treasuries* and also the *Imperially Endorsed Catalog of Xiqing Inkstones*. These record that the Qianlong Emperor had written words of commemoration for this stone several times, and note:

> "This *yanshan* is a rare treasure and has been owned by Mi Fu of the Song Dynasty and Zhao Mengfu of the Yuan Dynasty in succession, being passed down from generation to generation for over 600 years, with no erosion from wind and rain, as if blessed by heavenly beings."

Chi BiYang Chi Hong (Red Pond Reflecting Red Cliffs)
Red-silk stone *yanshan*, Shandong province
10 x 31 x 15 cm

Yanshan are normally not large, no more than one *chi* (about 33 cm, a little over a foot). None of the several *yanshan* in historical records are large, some no larger than the palm of the hand. Small as they are, they are able to embody majestic vistas, an attractive feature of stone appreciation reflected in such lines as "All the beauty of the misty rain and rising peaks is in the stone on my palm" by the renowned Song poet Su Shi (1037–1101) and "The scenery of a thousand kilometers is shown in a stone the size of my fist" by the well-known Tang poet Bai Juyi (772–846).

Red-silk Yanshan

Although Lingbi, Ying, Taihu, and Kun stones are traditionally the most highly regarded scholars' rocks, when it comes to inkstones, Red-silk stones rank first, followed by Duan, She, and Chengni stones. Only when in the later Song did Red-silk stone gradually become exhausted were Taihu stones included in the list of China's four major inkstones. According to *Yunlin Stone Catalogue* by Du Guan of the Song dynasty, Red-silk inkstones were considered best. Tang dynasty calligrapher Liu Gongquan (778–865) also said in an essay that Red-silk *yanshan* were his favorite.

Over the years, I have been fortunate enough to collect a number of excellent *yanshan*, one of which is a Song dynasty Red-silk inkstone with an ink basin (above). Although eroded at the bottom, it is well preserved as a whole. The rocks around the ink basin of various heights and not overly imposing, thus adding more space to the basin and presenting a sense of opennesss and tranquility.

The Red-silk *yanshan* above is unique in structure. The ink basin is on an upper level, like a heavenly pond, while underneath is a naturally formed deep cave, like a secret abode of Daoist immortals. The tiered structure presents a magical miniature world. Both *yanshan* are dark red, with moist rock, and ink traces at the edges of their basins affirming their former use as inkstones.

Tian Chi (Heavenly Pond)
Red-silk stone *yanshan*, Shandong province
9 x 22 x 15 cm

Xiang ZijingYanshan (Xiang Zijing's Yanshan)
Lingbi stone *yanshan,* Lingbi county, Anhui province
32 x 30 x 73 cm, 18th to 19th c Jiangnan style wooden stand

Xiang Zijing's Yanshan

Xiang Yuanbian (1525–1590), styled Zijing and also known as Molin, was a noted painter and connoisseur in the Ming dynasty. A Lingbi *yanshan* inscribed *Xiang Zijing Yanshan* owned by a Chicago collector in the 1970s has fluctuating ridges and peaks with crisscross gullies, dark and moist surface, with a thick natural patina (opposite). This *yanshan* fully exhibits the dynamism and diversity of a huge mountain range, with peaks, valleys, ravines, and twelve scenic spots, each inscribed with a name such as "Lotus Peak," "Radiant Cave," "Miraculous Sound Ravine," etc. Guided by the inscriptions, viewers' eyes can wander through the stone and appreciate these scenes. The two *yanshan* once owned by Emperor Li Yu and Mi Fu mentioned earlier also have such inscriptions, which are rare in *yanshan*.

This *Xiang Zijing Yanshan* has a natural bottom and can be laid flat. There are inscriptions on both on back and at bottom, showing that it originally did not have a wooden base. Before the Ming dynasty not every *yanshan* stone had a wooden base, which were normally custom made for the stones later. The high-waisted base of this *yanshan* is made of rosewood, graceful in shape and exquisite in workmanship.

Liu Yong's Yanshan

A Ying stone *yanshan* was inscribed *Xiangyang Wuyu* by the well-known scholar Liu Yong (1719–1804) during the reign of Emperor Qianlong. Also known as Shi'an, Liu Yong was a master of calligraphy, noted for the use of rich and moist ink in composing elegant and vigorous calligraphy. Xiangyang here refers to Mi Fu, who once lived in Xiangyang county of Hubei province, hence sometimes referred to as Mi Xiangyang; *wuyu* means "speechless." *Xiangyang Wuyu* means that even the great stone collector and scholar Mi Fu would be struck dumb by the magic and beauty of this *yanshan*, which boasts natural and breathtaking peaks and grotesque rocks. The exquisite wooden base made in the sixteenth or seventeenth centuries remains intact

A number of stories surround this *yanshan*, one of which relates that Liu Yong gave it to his daughter for her dowry, a story that appears to have no supporting evidence. Meanwhile, Liu Yong has become extremely popular recently as an honest and wise government official in a TV series *Prime Minister Liu Luoguo* (Luoguo was Liu's sobriquet) broadcast several years ago. Interestingly, this again raised curiosity about the whereabouts of the wonderful stone once in his possession. I confess as well to waiting many years news of its availability, and was fortunate to finally be able to acquire it.

Since *yanshan* are among the oldest collected stone types in China there are, of course, a huge numbers of excellent examples. Those I have collected over the years have been passed down through generations and each has a colorful story behind it. However, to keep this chapter reasonably brief I will limit myself to the few shown here.

Liu Yong Yanshan (Liu Yong's Yanshan)
Ying stone, Yingde county, Guangdong province
inscribed *"Xiangyang Wuyu"* and Liu's style name, *"Shi'an"*
30 x 22 x 18 cm, 16th to 17th c Ming style wooden stand

Above: *ShanYue Lian (Romance of Mountain and Moon)*
Lingbi stone *yanshan,* Lingbi county, Anhui province
32 x 29 x 9 cm, 17th to 18th c wooden stand

Opposite above: *Xiao Jiu Hua (Little Mount Jiu Hua)*
Lingbi stone *yanshan*, Lingbi county, Anhui province
16 x 14 x 10 cm, 16th to 17th c northern style wooden stand

Opposite below: *Wo Hu Shan (Sleeping Tiger Hill)*
Lingbi stone *yanshan*, Lingbi county, Anhui province
14 x 25 x 10 cm, 20th c wooden stand

Above: *Shun Lin Emei (Spring Arrives at Emei Mountain)*
Lingbi stone *yanshan,* Lingbi county, Anhui province
14 x 15 x 10 cm, 18th c Jiangnan style wooden stand

Yue Tai Xian Jing (Pinnacle Platform in a Wonderland)
Laoshan green stone yanshan, Shandong province
14 x 15 x 10 cm, 18th c Jiangnan style wooden stand

Above: *Qiu Shui Heng Bo (Autumn Water with Waves)*
Carved Lingbi stone *yanshan,* Lingbi county, Anhui province
11 x 14 x 4 cm, 19th to 20th c wooden stand

Opposite above: *Hui Yun (Converging Clouds)*
Lingbi stone *yanshan*, Lingbi county, Anhui province
8 x 4 x 5 cm, 20th c wooden stand

Opposite below: *Yu Shu Lin Feng (Charming Man Peak)*
Ying stone *yanshan*, Guangdong province
17 x 13 x 8 cm, 17th to 18th c marble stand

Left: *Mi Fu Bai Shi (Mi Fu Bows to a Rock)*
Yanshan, stone type unknown
15 x 11 x 6 cm, 18th to 19th c wooden stand

Above: *Hei Zhen Zhu (Black Pearl)*
Pearl Lingbi stone *yanshan,* Lingbi county, Anhui province
10 x 10 x 4 cm, 20th c wooden stand

Below: *Ling Feng Miao Jing (Celebration of Dancing Clouds)*
Lingbi stone *yanshan,* Lingbi county, Anhui province
8 x 14 x 5 cm, 19th c wooden stand

Above: *Chang Qing Yanshan (Chang Qing's Yanshan)*
Lingbi stone *yanshan*, Lingbi county, Anhui province
Inscribed *"Chang Qing,"* style name of Fan Xiu (1736–99)
6 x 12 x 4 cm, 19th c wooden stand

Below: *Mo Yu Fei Pu (Waterfall on Black Jade Hill)*
Black stone *yanshan,* from Yan mountain, near Beijing
5 x 12 x 4 cm, 19th c wooden stand

Dong Zhong Dong (Worlds Within Worlds)
Qingzhou stone, Qingzhou county, Shandong province
36 x 20 x 14 cm, 17th c or earlier wooden stand

In Search of Qingzhou Stones

Among Chinese collectors, four stone types have traditionally been considered the best: Lingbi stone, from Lingbi county in Anhui province; Ying stone, from Yingde county in Guangdong province; Taihu, a widely dispersed limestone associated with the lake of that name in Jiangsu province; and Kun stone, from the Yufeng mountain near the city of Kunshan, Jiangsu province. All are mentioned in the *Yunlin Stone Catalogue* of the Song dynasty and the *Suyuan Stone Catalogue* of the Ming dynasty. However, Qingzhou stone, which was mentioned in the *Yunlin Catalogue* after Lingbi stone, is relatively obscure and not mentioned at all in the *Suyuan Catalogue*. The mystery of this omission has persisted because no research has been done to shed light on it till now.

Qingzhou is located in today's Shandong province, but in the past was much larger, one of the nine *zhou* (an administrative division) of ancient China. The home of Confucius and Mencius, Shandong had fostered the largest number of *zhuang yuan*, scholars who ranked number one in imperial examinations. Consequently, it was regarded as a home of men of letters, among whom, as we have seen, collecting scholars' rocks was a popular pastime. Of the rare examples of ancient stones we can see today, the majority have been found in Shandong, the place referred to as Qingzhou in ancient times. These stones, aged, simple, and unsophisticated, are all fine works of nature that have been passed down from generation to generation for hundreds of years. Some of them produce resonant tones when struck and most are furnished with their original bases of the bulky, square style typically found in Shandong. However, is this what was meant by Qingzhou stones in the *Yunlin Catalogue?*

Shandong actually boasts a diversity of stone types; most representative and popular today are Laoshan green stone, found near the southeastern coast of the province; Boshan Wen stone, sometimes called simply Wen stone, found near Zibo city; and the Red-silk stone of Linqi and modern Qingzhou counties. (For more information on these stone types, see my *Modern Chinese Scholars' Rocks*.) In fact, Red-silk inkstones were also called Qingzhou inkstones in ancient times. Although all stone types harvested in Qingzhou might be considered Qingzhou stones, certainly not all of them are Qingzhou stones in the specific sense recorded in *Yunlin Catalogue*. We must assume

Feng Huai Lu Zhuan (Crooked Peaks With Myriad Detours)
Qingzhou stone, Qingzhou county, Shandong province
18 x 12 x 7 cm, 18th c wooden stand

the case is similar to that of Lingbi stone. Although in the broadest sense, all stones found in Lingbi county of Anhui province can be called Lingbi stones, the epithet "Number One Stone Under Heaven" is specifically reserved for stones taken from Shiqing Mountain. With respect to Qingzhou stones, according to the *Yunlin Stone Catalogue*:

> Qingzhou stones are found in the earth. The bigger ones are several *chi* [33 cm, a bit more than a foot] in size and the smaller ones about one *chi*. Some of them are only the size of a fist or simply pieces of rock that resemble nothing. [Yet] they are exquisite and far outnumber other stone types in the number of grottos in them. Most of the openings are stuffed with soft soil and when the soil is removed carefully with a bamboo branch, the stones show scattered purple color and reveal a slightly dry surface, with tiny passages burrowed in them, delicately connecting with each other. Usually they do not look like peaks and cliffs and produce no sound when tapped.

Judging from the above description, particularly from the "many grottos in the stones" and the "tiny passages . . . connecting with each other," Qingzhou stones are not among the types known from Shandong today. They are not described as dark purple, and seem distinctly different from any kind of Boshan Wen stone normally seen, most of which do have peaks and cliffs.

That being the case, what are the Qingzhou stones recorded in the *Yunlin Catalogue*? To answer this question, I researched related materials and consulted a number of experts over the years. However, their differing answers led to no satisfactory conclusion. It seems that most collectors have focused their attention on a certain kind of Wen stone that resembles Lingbi stone, even though this type is unlike the Qingzhou stones depicted in the *Yunlin Catalogue*.

In 2004 in Shanghai, I bought a wonderful ancient stone with numerous grottos intricately linked to one another. When fellow collectors saw it for the first time, none was sure what kind of stone it was, although since it had an old rectangular Shandong-

style base, I believed that it must have some connection with that province. In 2007 I had the opportunity to visit some stone lovers in Zibo city in Shandong, fortunately having brought with me a photo of my mystery stone. There, my hosts determined the stone of my picture was likely from the area of modern Qingzhou and Yidu counties in Shandong. When we then compared the picture carefully against the text of the *Yunlin Catalogue*, we were astonished to find how perfectly its description of Qingzhou stones fit. As described, the stone has many grottos or caves in it, which though not big, are connected with each other through irregular channels. We finally concluded that the ancient stone I collected several years ago was indeed one of, or very like the Qingzhou stones recorded in the *Yunlin Catalogue*. My journey to this discovery is aptly expressed by the ancient Chinese proverb, "Wearing out my iron shoes, I found it nowhere; yet making no effort one day, I obtained it." Since the Song dynasty, Qingzhou stones have become almost an extinct category. No wonder, since no one has been sure what they really look like.

NINE WONDERFUL STONES

Apart from scholars' stones with well-recorded histories, there are many ancient stones with no documentation at all but likely with equally interesting stories behind them. For example, *Mulan's Peak* (right) may appear at first glance to be a Lingbi stone due to its smooth and dark surface. It is, in fact, a Taihu stone blackened with smoke, a process devised by stone purveyors of the early Ming dynasty when the more precious Lingbi stones were in short supply. This chapter contains examples of extraordinary stones that have been passed down through many generations to the present day and are deserving of our attention. In this chapter, I have chosen to introduce nine ancient stones, through which I hope both to clarify points of observation and connoisseurship discussed in previous writings, and to share with fellow collectors, new and experienced, some thoughts about the pleasures of stone collecting.

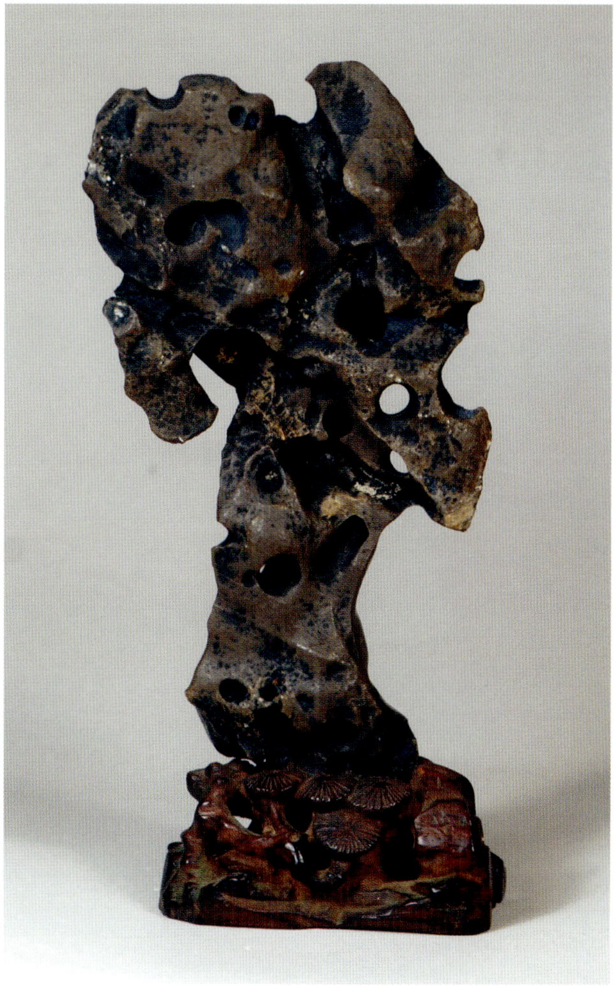

Opposite above: *Shan Gao Yue Xiao (From a Tall Mountain, a Small Moon)*
Ying stone, Guangdong province
12 x 13 x 6 cm, 19th c wooden stand

Opposite below: *Xiao Dai Yue (Little Dai and Two Peaks of Taishan)*
Yan stone, Yan Mountain, near Beijing
7 x 8 x 5 cm, 19th c wooden stand

Mulan Feng (Mulan's Peak)
Taihu stone, Jiangsu province
17 x 8 x 5 cm, 19th c open style wooden stand

Wen Shi Xiong Feng (Majestic Peak)
Boshan Wen stone, Shandong province
72 x 8 x 8 cm, 19th c southern style wooden stand

Majestic Peak

Boshan Wen stone

This gray scholars' rock with its craggy peak is majestic and imposing, recalling what Su Shi of the Song dynasty wrote: "A good stone should exhibit *xiong* as well as *wen*." *Xiong* refers to a quality of majesty, not necessarily reflected in size but in the embodiment of an extraordinary power and dynamism. *Wen* refers to literary grace, an elegance that can be embodied in natural objects as well as man-made artistic creations. Normally, the surfaces of Boshan Wen stones are wrinkled, occasionally containing holes and rarely channels. This stone contains not only holes, but also twelve channels of different sizes, imparting a sense of hidden mysteries and infinite internal variations. Also it is naturally formed and produces a resonance upon being struck.

What also deserves attention is that although this Boshan Wen stone came from Shandong province it rests on a carved wooden base of Guangdong style, an anomaly not often found in ancient scholars' rocks. Although this may seem a trivial detail, the true stone connoisseur will trace the history of a stone not only from its origins, composition, color, patina, and aesthetic qualities, but also from the material and carving style of its wooden base. A careful collector of his particular stone would want to know: Did a carver from Guangdong create the base for this stone in Shandong, or was the stone sent to Guangdong for a base? Since the stone was finally found in Beijing, did someone move or ship the fairly large piece (72 cm in height) from Shandong to Guangdong and then to Beijing?

One begins to imagine various scenarios: the stone might have been owned by a stone collector in Shandong until he left for Guangdong due to a political appointment, common in the career of scholar officials. There, he might have asked a local carver to make a wooden base, retaining the rectangular shape of the stone base but with Guangdong style carving. The collector might later have been called to an appointment in the capital, Beijing. Or perhaps in Guangdong a visiting Beijing official might have admired and acquired this stone, which finally traveled a huge distance to settle in Beijing. It may sound far-fetched, but we have noted Shandong as the home province of many successful scholar-officials. Service in the economically vital southern province of Guangdong could be a normal step in a government career that was concluded at the capital. If the stone could speak, it would certainly reveal more colorful details.

The fact remains that very few scholars' rocks from Shangdong have wooden bases with such rich and elegant carving. The most obvious explanation for this and for the stone's lengthy sojourn from Shandong to Guangdong to Beijing is that its owner, certainly a person of high social status, took the stone as an intimate friend to be with at all times.

Wen Shi Xiong Feng (Majestic Peak), two additional views
Boshan Wen stone, Shandong province
72 x 8 x 8 cm, 19th c southern style wooden stand

Little Miraculous Peak of Song

Lingbi stone

This stone is natural in shape, dark in color, and moist in appearance. Shiny as leather, it is a graceful and elegant peak showing the characteristics valued in stones of the Song dynasty. When appreciating ancient scholars' rocks, connoisseurs will first look at the stone's natural patina and its wooden base. The former normally falls into two categories, either dry or moist. Dry patina is formed by oxidization by air or by erosion by water, leaving the surface grayish and rough. Moist patina characterizes the surface of well-handled stones, which are smoothed by the natural oils of the hands over a long period of caressing by collectors. Among such stones, Lingbi stones exhibit the most prominently moist patina.

The earliest Lingbi stones appeared after mountain landslides and torrents washed away the surrounding soil, exposing the underground stones. Exposed to the elements for thousands more years, washed by water and natural forces year after year, these stones turned dark black and acquired their characteristic moist surfaces and peculiar shapes. Discovered by locals, they were sold to men of letters who came to prize and to collect them. A well-known story about the Song collector Mi Fu relates how, in response to a a criticism from his superior, Inspector Yang, that he wasted too much time admiring stones, he pulled three small, fine stones from his sleeve one by one (*Scholars' Rocks,* p 25). From the description recorded, these were Lingbi stones, and their beauty ended the remonstration; Inspector Yang snatched the best stone and drove off in his cart.

These first Lingbi stones were of small size, with wonderfully idiosyncratic shapes and moist surfaces.

Due partly to the polish of nature and partly to the caresses of stone collectors, these ancient stones became smooth, mellow, and often with patinas resembling dark leather. Only later, when such stones could not be collected on the surface, did the digging of Lingbi stones begin, yielding stones with less naturally stunning qualities. Interestingly, a natural patina is not easily to be preserved on Lingbi stones; a stone that has been kept but not often handled for a hundred years may appear almost the same as a newly harvested stone. It is worth mentioning that this *Little Miraculous Peak* is one of the Lingbi stones in this book that has the thickest moist patina.

Scholars' rocks in the Song dynasty typically did not have wooden bases; the bases they are displayed on today were all fashioned for them in the Ming and Qing dynasties. No one knows through how many generations this *Little Miraculous Peak* has been passed down, or how many cities in China it has visited. Judging from the present wooden base, however, it once resided in Shanxi province, as evidenced by two coin-like carvings on each side. decorative motifs in other parts of China. During the Ming and Qing dynasties, Shanxi was noted for as a place where government and businessmen cooperated most closely and such coin-shaped motifs were popular, including on wooden bases for stones.

Song Keng Xiao Shen Feng (Little Miraculous Peak of Song)
Lingbi stone, Lingbi county, Anhui province
9 x 12 x 16 cm, 18th to 19th c Shanxi style wooden stand

Willow Spring Stone

Lingbi stone

This stone was purportedly acquired from someone who worked at the Museum of Pu Songling during the period of the Cultural Revolution (1966–1976), implying that a previous owner of the stone had been Pu Songling (1640–1715), a well-known novelist from Shandong province during the Qing dynasty. A fervent stone lover, Pu Songling composed many poems and stories about his favorite stones; among them one titled *Shi Qing Xu*, or *Ethereal Rock*, appears in his masterpiece *Strange Tales from a Chinese Studio* (*Liaozhai Zhiyi*). This well-known tale is about a stone lover whose favorite stone is grabbed away by a rich and powerful scoundrel but who finally gets it back through great effort. Pu Songling has come to be recognized among collectors as one of the greatest stone lovers of the Qing Dynasty. Currently, there remain two scholars rocks in the museum, the *Hai Yue Shi (Sea and Mountain Stone)* and

Opposite: *Liu Quan (Willow Spring)*
Inscribed on back *"Liu Quan"* (above) and signed *"Shou Zhuo"*
Lingbi stone, Lingbi county, Anhui province
52 x 32 x 22 cm, 17th to 18th c northern style wooden stand

Hai Yue Shi (Sea and Mountain Stone)
Lingbi stone, Lingbi county, Anhui province
34 x 62 x 25 cm, 18th to 19th c wooden stand, Memorial Residence of Pu Songling, Zibo City, Shandong province

the *Wa Ming Shi (Frog Croaking Stone)*, both believed to have been donated in his name by a close friend.

Because Pu Songling was also known as the Liu Quan Hermit, and the stone is inscribed "*Liu Quan*" at the lower back, it is thought to have belonged to him. Yet when I first saw this stone and considered its purported history, I immediately arrived at the conclusion that it did not belong to Pu Songling. My reasons are as follows:

Though this Lingbi stone has no holes in it, it is in the shape of a Buddha's hand and appears heavy and solid. Moreover, it has a dark black and moist surface, a thick natural patina, and a rectangular wooden base of high-quality workmanship. All these qualities indicate that this rock was a valuable work belonging to a noted, probably wealthy, collector. Pu Songling, on the other hand, lived a poor and simple life, working as a private tutor in his friend Bi Youji's home most of the latter's life of about thirty years. It is completely unlikely that he personally could afford to own such a stone. In fact, the two well-known stones in his museum were donations of the Bi family.

Secondly, although Pu Songling is famous for his writing, he is not noted for his calligraphy and carving skills. The two characters for the name *Liu Quan*

Illustration of Shi Qing Xu (Ethereal Rock)
from *Liaozhai Zhiyi (Strange Tales from a Chinese Studio)*
by Pu Songling (1640–1715)

at the bottom of the stone are in Lishu script, square and strong, and showing great calligraphic skill. They are certainly the work of a prominent calligrapher and carver.

The final reason will be obvious to those familiar with Chinese signatures and colophons on artworks. Because Pu Songling was himself the so-called Willow Spring Hermit, the two characters *Liu Quan* should appear at the place of his signature; however, they appear instead on the lower back of the stone. In the place of signature is the name *Shou Zhuo,* meaning "clumsy self," a term used by many scholars in ancient China to express their humility, going back as early as Tao Yuanming (365–427) of the Jin dynasty. Further research is therefore needed to identify the master calligrapher who inscribed the name *Shou Zhou* at the bottom of this stone.

Judging from its wooden base, the stone must have been owned by a collector in Shandong province, where most of the stones collected were Wen, Qingzhou, or Laoshan green stones, very few being Lingbi stones.

Twin-Peak Stone

Stone type unknown

Although its origin is unknown, the simple but generously proportioned wooden base shows that this stone may have come from Shandong province, while the glossy stone surface tells us that it was once washed by water. The lower part of this stone has a bold shape with the upper part taking the form of two peaks facing each other. To some viewers this stone fully expresses the central tenet permeating Asian philosophy and religion: that of a fundamental unity (e.g., the Dao), manifesting itself in the universe as a dualism (e.g., *yin* and *yang*), whose interaction gives rise to the "myriad things" we perceive with our senses. Appreciating this stone can lead one to profound and lengthy meditation on how these wonderful mechanisms of creation can operate in unison, simultaneously, and without contradiction.

Judging from its smooth surface, this stone must have been taken from the water, and may be indicative of another source of interesting scholars' stones—China's coastal waters. Shandong province is a peninsularwith a long coastline and was also the source of the very desirable Laoshan green stones, which were sometimes referred to as "sea bottom jade" (*haidi yu*, see *MCSC*, p. 37). A poem by Su Shi (1037–1101) contains the following lines: "As I return with this stone / in my sleeve is the Eastern Sea," referring to the waters off the Shandong peninsula. In an essay "Notes on Twelve Stones from the North Sea," Su Shi mentions that Wu Ziye (1004–1069), one of the "eight worthies in Chaozhou," collected twelve strange stones in the waters off Dengzhou (present Penglai City in Shandong province) with the help of the local magistrate and other officials; he then had them shipped them to Sui-Han Hall, his studio in Guangdong province. In concluding his essay, Su Shi writes: "Though the world abounds in stone lovers, very few have carried stones from the North Sea to the South Sea."

The *Suyuan Stone Catalogue* includes this essay by Su Shi and illustrates it with drawings of the twelve stones. However, since there is a lapse of about six centuries between Su Shi and Lin Youlin, author of

Shuang Feng Qi Shi (Twin Peaks)
Stone type unknown
47 x 41 x 17 cm, 15th c northern style wooden stand

Left: *Bi Ling HengYun (Green Cliff amidst Wafting Clouds)*
Laoshan green stone, Shandong province
26 x 26 x 13 cm, 19th c northern style wooden stand

Bi Shan Ru Zui (Intoxicating Green Mountain)
Laoshan green stone, Shandong province
41 x 15 x 13 cm, 19th to 20th c wooden stand

the *Suyuan Catalogue*, we must be suspicious about the authenticity of these images. Still, it is generally acknowledged that collection of sea stones was popular in the Song dynasty. After the Song dynasty, there were few records of stones taken from the Shandong coast, except Laoshan green stones.

Still, if this *Twin Peak Stone* with its thick natural patina was indeed taken from the coastal waters off Shandong in the Song dynasty and passed town to our time, we must indeed count ourselves fortunate. One can only hope that similar stones with more clues as to their origins may yet be found, which would greatly benefit research on China's ancient scholars' rocks.

Left: *Du Hai Guanyin (Guanyin Crossing the Sea)*
Laoshan green stone, Shandong province
25 x 11 x 7 cm, 19th to 20th c wooden stand

SuiYue Liu Hua (Majesty Produced by Time)
Laoshan green stone, Shandong province
26 x 14 x 9 cm, 15th to 17th c wooden stand

Cave Heaven, Auspicious Land

Lingbi stone

This stone is remarkable for its original base, also made of stone. It has three peaks of varying heights on an upper level, with three naturally formed caves below, with two of the caves connected to each other. *Dong tian fu di* literally means "Cave heaven, Auspicious Land," a reference to Daoist realms. According to Daoist tenets, a d*ong tian* is a heavenly abode populated by immortals, while a *fu di* is a land of pure happiness. There are ten major *dong tian*, thirty-six minor *dong tian*, and seventy-two *fu di*. Together, they refer to paradises free of worldly vexations and struggles for power and fortune. These utopia were imagined by scholar officials, weary of the coarseness and corruption surrounding them. Contemplation of such scholars' rocks allowed them to travel vicariously to happier places and escape the vulgar world, if only for a brief time.

Parts of this stone are covered with thin layers of earthen residue that have not been washed away, indicating that it was buried underground for a long period. This might have resulted from a funeral observance or perhaps natural disaster after being collected. Yet other parts exhibit a thick and dark natural patina, testifying to the fact that before burial the stone had been kept by some collector(s) for a long time. Judging by the stone's shape and patina, it might date from the Song dynasty.

The base of this wonderful stone is carved of Yuzi stone. Very few ancient scholars' rocks have original bases of stone, a difficult medium to carve and not easy to repair when mistakes are made. However, stone bases were fashioned for scholars' stones prior to the Ming, but this is not always the case. From the Ming dynasty onward, bases have normally been made of wood. Of the four stones with stone bases in my collection, this one is the plainest and simplest, reflecting a coherent style, and attesting to a long history of collection.

Dong Tian Fu Di (Cave Heaven, Auspicious Land)
Lingbi stone, Lingbi county, Anhui province
48 x 24 x 22 cm, 15th c or earlier stone stand

> Gazing at the Summit
>
> How can one describe Tai Mountain,
> Its vast greenness towering above Chi and Lu?
> Here is creation's sacred beauty
> Its north and south slopes dividing dusk
> from dawn.
> Chest heaving, one reaches the birthplace of
> clouds
> Vision blinded by flocks of returning birds.
> Someday I must climb to the peak
> To behold all mountains in a single glance.

All Mountains in a Single Glance

Boshan Wen stone

The name of this stone is a loose translation of *Yi lan zhong shan xiao*, literally "One / glance / myriad / mountains / small," the well-known concluding line of a poem by Du Fu (712–772) of the Tang dynasty. The poem, *Wang Yue* (*Gazing at the Summit*) recounts or imagines a climb to the summit of the sacred mountain Tai Shan, from which all other mountains would appear small enough to be seen in a single glance. This stone resembles a bird soaring high above the earth and thus affording a view similar to that from the summit of Tai Shan.

Although the shape of most ancient stones calls to mind natural scenery, only a few resemble specific flora and fauna, and even fewer are as naturally dynamic and vivid as this one. Moreover, this stone boasts an extraordinarily dramatic shape. While most bird-shaped stones need a wooden base to elevate them and enhance their dynamism, this one is exceptional, with both wings widely extended and a long and slim lower body, together giving a powerful impression of soaring into the heavens.

Most scholars' rocks provoke in viewers profound thoughts or induce a meditative state or feeling of tranquility. Others such as this one, rarer in number, convey an impression of movement and excitement that stimulates and inspires. Descriptions of similarly dynamic scholars' appear in ancient records. An essay titled "Zhenjiang Stone" in the *Suyuan Catalogue* says, "There is a really peculiar stone in Zhenjiang that is full of momentum. It is dark purple in color and looks moist and well-nourished."

This Boshan Wen stone has an abundance of veins on the surface, with mostly diagonal crisscrossing striations all over. Boasting a dramatically undulating shape, it is covered with thick natural patina. It can be viewed from any side and produces resonant tone upon striking. This stone has a base carved out of another stone type, which from a distance appears to be wood.

Yi Lan Zhong Shan Xiao (All Mountains in a Single Glance)
Boshan Wen stone, Shandong province
46 x 42 x 28 cm, 17th to18th c stone stand

The Thinker

Ying stone

This Ying stone is both bright and dark in places, with thick natural patina and dots all over the surface giving the impression of antiquity. The English name for this stone is borrowed from that of the well-known sculpture of Auguste Rodin (1840–1917) now in the Musée Rodin in Paris. It is hoped this clearly conveys some sense of its Chinese names, either *Chan Ding*, meaning "cultivating the mind" or *Jing Si*, meaning "meditation." To various viewers it appears to be a Buddhist monk sitting in silent meditation, or a wise man engaged in lofty contemplation, or even an elderly person lost in a nostalgic reverie. Whichever of these or another image is conveyed depends upon how each viewer approaches it. However, in any case we participate in the irony presented by Rodin's work: we find ourselves contemplating one engaged in contemplation. Another distinctive feature of this stone is its deliberately lofty two-tiered base, which reflects the respect due to the seated figure, whether a monk or an elderly lay person.

It is often the case that the same stone can provoke different feelings and reactions in different viewers and even in the same viewer at different times. I have chosen to present this stone not only because its unique shape deserves mention, but because it clearly illustrates the breadth in interpretation possible in stone appreciation, the ability of a single stone to conjure up different images.

Jing Si (The Thinker)
Ying stone, Yingde county, Guangdong province
47 x 30 x 19 cm, 19th c wooden stand

YiYun Feng (Leisurely Cloud Pinnacle)
Ying stone, Yingde county, Guangdong province
47 x 30 x 19 cm, 18th to 19th c Jiangnan style wooden stand

明治四十年二月七日

Left: Sheet of the *Osaska Mainichi Shimbun (Osaka Daily News)* from box in which *Leisurely Cloud Pinnacle* was packed
Below: Box with lid marked *ling shi (spirit stone)*

Leisurely Cloud Pinnacle

Ying stone

This superb creation of nature appears dark and craggy, elegant and austere, its features enhanced by an exquisite rosewood stand. This stone was once kept in Japan and on its wooden case are the two characters *ling shi*, meaning "spirit stone." A 1907 Osaka *Mainichi Shimbun* (*Daily News*) was among the old newspapers used to pack the box, leading one to believe the stone was in Japan at that time. Chinese scholars' rocks were first brought to Japan by eminent Chinese monks visiting during the Tang and Song dynasty, when Chinese Buddhism was becoming very widespread in Japan. The stones were kept mainly in well-known Japanese temples, by the imperial family, and by other distinguished families. In *Inheritance Stones,* written and published by Sadasuke in 1967, eleven well-known Chinese stones in Japan are introduced, the most famous of which is a stone titled *A Floating Bridge of Dreams* (p. 80), collected by the Japanese Emperor, Go Daigo (1288–1339).

The Ying stone and Yellow Wax stones illustrated on pages 83–84 were owned by a Mr. Toyohara, who, according to his daughter, bought them from a well-known Japanese family in Kyoto in the 1960s. Later, Mr. Toyohara moved to Los Angeles and kept these stones for near fifty years. Ms. Toyohara told me that her father admired these stones all his life. It is a great honor for me to have some stones from his collection following his death in 2008.

Above: *Luofu Shan (Luofu Mountain)*
Stone type unknown, collected during the Tang dynasty
21 x 30 x 12 cm, Nezu Museum, Tokyo

Opposite: *Yu Shi Feng (Imperial Envoy Peak)*
Ying stone, Yingde county, Guangdong province
69 x 46 x 31 cm, 19th c wooden stand

Yume no Ukihashi (Floating Bridge of Dreams)
Ningshan stone, Jiangsu province
Collected by Emperor Go Daigo of Japan (1288–1339)
21 x 30 x 12 cm, The Tokugawa Art Museum, Nagoya

Left: *Yun Shang Jian Feng (Sword Peak above the Clouds)*
Ying stone, Yingde county, Guangdong province
76 x 30 x 16 cm, 19th c open southern style wooden stand

Opposite above: *Untitled*
Yellow wax stone, Guangdong province
10 x 29 x 18 cm, 19th c open southern style wooden stand

Opposite below: *Untitled*
Yellow wax stone, Guangdong province
17 x 32 x 18 cm, 19th c open southern style wooden stand

Elegant and Magnificent Peak

Artificial stone

Tai Xiu Hua (Elegant and Magnificent Peak)
Yixing ceramic scholars' stone, Jiangsu province
40 x 14 x 10 cm, 18th to 19th c wooden stand

Although this appears to be a Lingbi stone, it is in fact an artificial creation made of *zisha*, or "purple sand," a fine clay which comes from Yixing in Jiangsu province. Its use in ceramics dates back to the Song dynasty and is well known to collectors of Yixing pottery. Scholars and stone collectors throughout the dynasties took a fancy to works of art that simulated stones, including replicas fashioned from jade, wood, tree root, porcelain, glass, and copper, as well as Shoushan stone, a type of alabaster easily carved with natural scenes. Throughout Chinese history, whenever the economy prospered stone collection would become increasingly popular and so encourage production of artworks resembling stones. In seeking out fine stones, a collector today may encounter what appears to be an ordinary small Ying stone, but upon

Elegant and Magnificent Peak

Artificial stone

Tai Xiu Hua (Elegant and Magnificent Peak)
Yixing ceramic scholars' stone, Jiangsu province
40 x 14 x 10 cm, 18th to 19th c wooden stand

Although this appears to be a Lingbi stone, it is in fact an artificial creation made of *zisha*, or "purple sand," a fine clay which comes from Yixing in Jiangsu province. Its use in ceramics dates back to the Song dynasty and is well known to collectors of Yixing pottery. Scholars and stone collectors throughout the dynasties took a fancy to works of art that simulated stones, including replicas fashioned from jade, wood, tree root, porcelain, glass, and copper, as well as Shoushan stone, a type of alabaster easily carved with natural scenes. Throughout Chinese history, whenever the economy prospered stone collection would become increasingly popular and so encourage production of artworks resembling stones. In seeking out fine stones, a collector today may encounter what appears to be an ordinary small Ying stone, but upon

Above: *Two Yixing Teacups*
Zishan pottery, Yixing city, Jiangsu province
Left: 7 x 12 cm; right: 4 x 12 cm

Kunlun Shan (Kunlun Mountains)
Pottery scholars' stone, Fujian province
110 x 56 x 25 cm, 19th to 20th c wooden stand

more careful observation may find that it is a piece of fired ceramic. In fact, ancient fired stones may be even more valuable than real stones due to their scarcity, especially those made of the purple sand.

It is notable that although the artist who created this stone was free to fashion as many intricate holes as possible, he chose to restrain the number in order that it might look as closely as possible like a natural Lingbi stone. Its elegantly carved original wooden base attests to the learning and cultivation of its maker and to the high value placed upon it. The stone is called *Tai Xiu Hua* in memory of Zhao Zhi'ang, a well-known painter and stone collector of the Yuan dynasty (1271–1368). As Lin Youlin records in his *Suyuan Catalogue*, Zhao Zhi'ang had a stone of this name "with dark green scales faintly visible on the top, at the bottom and on the back. It is an integral whole and when placed on the table, it appears to be a man of virtue." Though this artificial stone looks like the elegant and magnificent peak of its namesake, it stands boldly upright like a man of virtue as well.

My collection includes two large peaks made of earthenware, both over one meter in height; one is dark gray and the other reddish gray. They had been kept in Daoist temples since the Ming dynasty or even before, documentation of their exact dates will require more research. As Daoists normally worship mountains, they also held stones in high esteem, considering them representatives of mountains. However, excellent mountain-shaped stones were not always available, and therefore were recreated in earthenware. These two stones present magnificent peaks, complete with valleys, cliffs, steep slopes, and caves, and were revered by Daoists for their representation of the "cave heavens" and "blessed lands" discussed earlier. One of them has a place in to burn incense for Daoist rituals.

Xi Zhao Qiu Shan (Afternoon Sunshine in Autumn Mountains)
Pottery scholars' stone, Fujian province
110 x 40 x 28 cm, 19th to 20th c wooden stand

Mountain-Shaped Incense Burner (Boshan Xianglu)
Chinese, 1st century BCE / AD. Bronze 21.3 x 19.4 cm dia. Lucy Maud Buckingham Collection, 1926.1864, The Art Institute of Chicago.

A Treasure from the Han Dynasty

In May of 2007, I went to Zibo city, Shandong province, to investigate the possible relationship between the Boshan Wen stones from that area and the somewhat similar Qingzhou stones described in the *Yunlin Stone Catalogue*. There I traveled with a local stone collector, Sun Zhaojun, to explore Boshan (Bo Mountain), the origin of the stones. Though I once had read an article about a rare stone in Mr. Sun's collection purportedly dating from the time of Emperor Wu of the Western Han dynasty (206 BCE–24 CE), I did not pay much attention to it, for I felt the chances too slim that such an object could be handed down for over two millennium until the present day. Mr. Sun had acquired the stone in 2005 from a Mr. Li, whose family had owned it for successive generations since the Qianlong era of the Qing dynasty (1736–95). At Mr. Sun's home, however, I was fortunate enough to see not only the actual stone but, more importantly, a copy of the *Genealogy of the Li Family* that accompanied it. This remarkable document consists of five volumes and includes poems and testimonials in praise of the stone by well-known scholar-officials. All attest to the fact that stone was indeed collected in the Western Han dynasty, and was subsequently known as the *Han Stone* or *Yi Nan* (literally "facilitate male") *Stone*. It was considered to be miraculous: women who prayed to it were believed more likely to bear male children.

Emperor Wu of the Han (156–87 BCE), also known as Han Wudi and whose personal name was Liu Che, was the seventh emperor of the dynasty, ascending to power in 141 BCE at age fifteen. During his reign the territory of China was vastly expanded, with trade opened to the west via the so-called Silk Roads. Considered one of the greatest of Chinese emperors, there exist copious historical records and a wealth of wonderful legends of Wudi's reign. Nearly contemporary accounts of his reign may be found the dynastic history *Han Shu* by Ban Gu (32–92 CE), translated by Homer H. Dubs as *History of the Former Han Dynasty* (Waverly Press, 1938–55).

According to the *Han Shu*, in the fall of 120 BCE, the Emperor reduced the garrisons at three frontier towns by half and put them to work excavating the Kunming Pond at the capital city of Chang'an (now Xian, in Shaanxi province). As well, "reprobate" officials were put to work digging the pond and cutting brush in the surrounding imperial Shanglin Park. The comprehensive Chinese dictionary *Ci Hai* explains:

> The Kunming Pond was originally a lowland area in the southeast of Doumen in Xi'an, Shaanxi province. It was created in 120 BCE, partly for drilling the navy in preparation for a war with the state of Kunming and partly to solve a water shortage in Chang'an. The pond, which extended forty miles when the excavation was finished, began to dry up after the dikes broke down during the reign of Emperor Taihe of the Tang, and gradually reverted to farmland after the Song dynasty.

A later commentator on the *Han Shu* (Fu Can, third century CE) noted that the Kunming Pond replicated a lake near Kunming, in today's Yunnan province, on which a naval battle was expected to take place during the planned invasion of that state. The King of Kunming had apparently offended Wudi by interfering with his envoys en route to India.

During the excavation, two strange stones were purportedly unearthed, dubbed "male" and "female." The reason for these names is unknown, but soon afterward the power to promote the birth of male children was ascribed to the female stone. The extant, purportedly female, *Kunming Stone* looks, according to the *Genealogy of the Li Family*, like "a dragon holding its head high and swimming underwater or like a predator crouching on the ground." Not a large stone, it is described as about one *chi* (about one foot) in height, "dark in color, with two white veins, resembling a bent old man." The power of the stone to facilitate the birth of boys is compared to that of the *lan cao*, which may be a type of orchid or lily but has not been positively indentified; it was believed that a woman who carried the plant during her pregnancy would bear a male child.

Other stone artworks are associated with the Kunming Pond and were placed on display around the shoreline. Two of these were dubbed the Herd Boy and Weaving Girl stones, named after two truly star-crossed lovers in Chinese mythology. When the Weaving Girl, whose job was to provide clothing for the immortals in heaven, neglected her duties out of her love for the Herd Boy, their punishment was to be banished to separate places in the night sky, seen by us mortals as the stars Altair and Vega. However, the gods later took pity on them, and once a year, on the seventh day of the seventh month, cause

Kunming Shi (Kunming Stone) aka *Yi Nan Shi (Facilitate Male Stone)*
Stone type unknown, Shaanxi province
40 x 42 x 20 cm, 20th c wooden stand

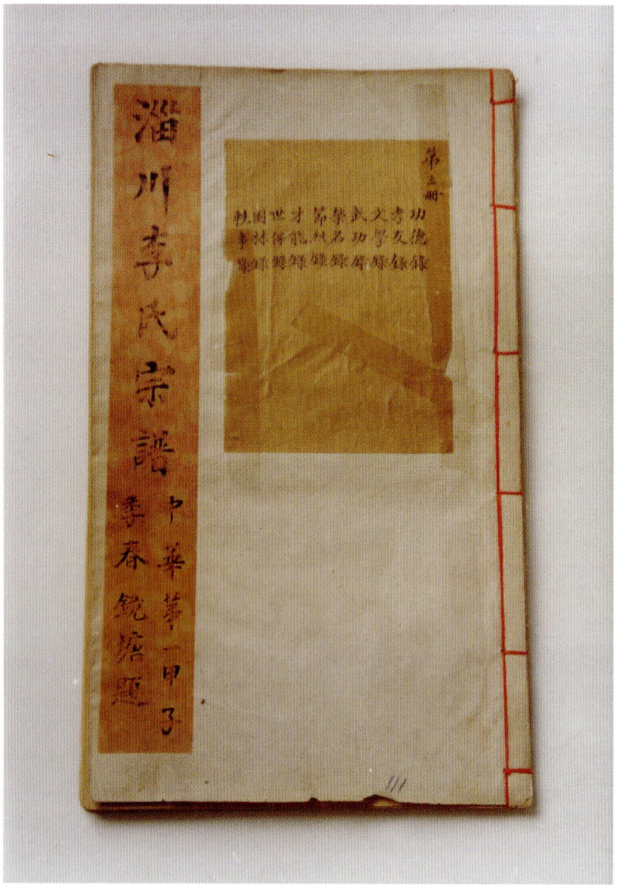

Zi Chuan Li Shi Zong Pu (Genealogy of the Li Family of Zi Chuan)
Volume 3 of 1924 edition
16 x 28 cm

a host of magpies to form a bridge over the gulf between them, so that the lovers can be reunited. It is unknown, however, whether the so-called Herd Boy and Weaving Girl stones were natural formations or sculptures. And finally there was reportedly a large stone fish placed at the Kunming Pond said to have miraculous powers: its scales would ripple and fins flap at the onset of stormy weather.

These several stories are linked together in a lovely poem titled *The Weaving Girl Stone of Kunming Pond* by Tang poet Tong Hanqing (n.d.):

A piece of rock from Kunming Pond,
For ages has been called the Weaving Girl
 stone.
Her soft eyes exude tenderness and love.
While her form appears more beautiful
 against the water.
Moss covering the stone appears a
 diaphanous gown,
The gentle waves of the pond sound like
 shuttles in her loom.
She exchanges smiles with the lotus flowers,
Her state of the mind so calm and peaceful,
Watching birds are never startled.
Like a reflection in a mirror,
She is mirrored in the pond,
A watery image lovely as the maiden herself.

Li Family Home
Bo Shan (formerly Zi Chuan), Shandong province
Photo courtesy of the Li family, 2009

Although we cannot know if the poet drew from personal observation, it is quite possible that the scene described could still be viewed in Tong Hanqing's day. This would accord with historical accounts, which report that dikes supporting Kunming Pond were severely damaged during the Tang, which witnessed the tumultuous upheaval of the An Lushan Rebellion (755–63). Or perhaps the environs were already in a state of disrepair, as there is no mention of a Herd Boy—they are usually referenced as a pair—or other remarkable stone.

Unfortunately, documentation of our *Kunming Stone* contains a gap of about 1200 years. When purchased by Li Shubai in the eighteenth century, it supposedly came with records tracing its origins to the Western Han, all subsequently lost. The available documentation, chronicling the stone before its possession by the Li family, is only what was copied into the family genealogy. Below are these testimonials, ranging over several dynasties, the earliest by Wang Dingguo, a noted scholar of the Northern Song (960–1127). After these, we will return to our consideration of whether the present *Kunming Stone* could really be the "female stone" excavated from the Kunming Pond during the Han dynasty.

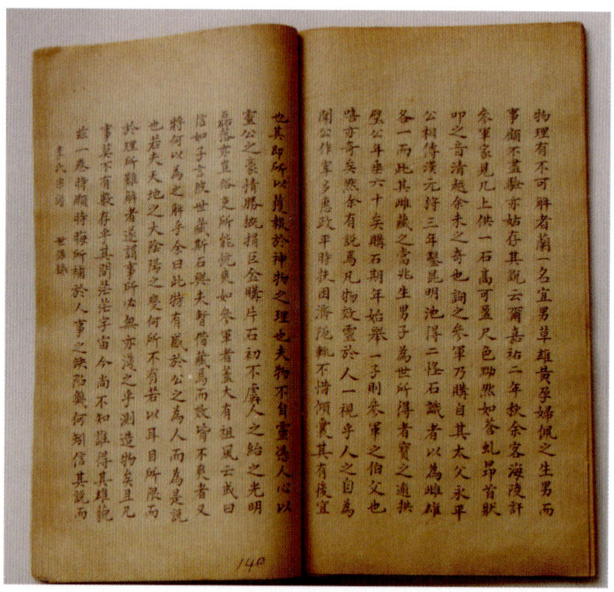

Note on the Kunming Stone
by Wang Dingguo (1048–after 1104)
from the *Geneology of the Li Family*

Note on the Kunming Stone

Wang Dingguo, autumn of 1079, in Linchuan

In nature, there are always things beyond human interpretation. Take, for example, the *lan cao*. It is said that a pregnant woman will give birth to a male child if she carries the plant during her pregnancy, but this is certainly not true in all cases, so let us dismiss it as a wild legend for the time being.

In the autumn of the second year of the reign of Jiayou [1057], I was at Administrator Xu's residence in Hailing [now Taizhou, Jiangsu province] for a visit, when I saw a peculiar stone on a long table. It was about one foot in height and dark in color, appearing like a dragon raising its head and producing a clear and resonant sound when tapped. However, I was not overly astonished by its peculiarity then. When I inquired of Administrator Xu about this stone, I was told that it was purchased and collected by his grandfather, Lord Yongping.

Legend has it that in the third year of the *yuanshou* reign of the Han dynasty [120 BCE], workers digging the Kunming Pond unearthed two strange stones. According to some stone connoisseurs, one of them was "male" and the other "female" and if people made offerings to the female stone, they would be blessed with a male child. Therefore, the stone was considered a priceless treasure. When Lord Yongping bought the stone, he was already nearly sixty years old. His wife then bore him a son, who was the uncle of Administrator Xu. This really sounded miraculous!

However, some say that whether a natural object can actually produce miraculous events for someone depends on that person's own character. It is said that when Lord Yongping served in the position of Prime Minister, he was honest and upright and implemented policies that benefited ordinary people. Moreover, he was extremely generous in aiding the poor and needy. Therefore, it is only natural that he should have sons sent by heaven.

In fact, natural objects alone are not efficacious. They make their presence felt only to one who has a kind heart and does good deeds. When Lord Yongping bought this stone with large sums of money, he did not worry about being cheated. His honorable state of mind was beyond reproach.

Administrator Xu, like his grandfather, believed that the stone would make its presence felt. Lord Yongping and later owners of the stone all had their desires fulfilled. Can there be a logical explanation for this? Some said that the stone owners attributed miracles to the stone because they admired Lord Yongping's honorable conduct.

The universe, as we can see, is vast and everything in it so changeable. There is indeed nothing that is impossible. Those who believe only what they see or hear and deny the existence of what they cannot see or hear are short-sighted, and underestimate the power of nature. Most of the things in the world have their own laws and man cannot even fathom the full extent and content of the vast universe. There are some who believe that this piece of stone can make up for their regrets but cannot afford it, while others who can afford it are afraid to do so. This is Heaven's will! Without the witty remarks and poems and inscriptions of the literatus Dongfang Shuo [154–93 BCE], Emperor Wu of the Western Han might have remained obscure. The story of this stone shows that there is a certain destiny in the unseen world that man cannot defy.

Administrator Xu's given name is Zhang, his courtesy name Huiting, his pseudonym Zilan, and is sometimes called Canglangzi.

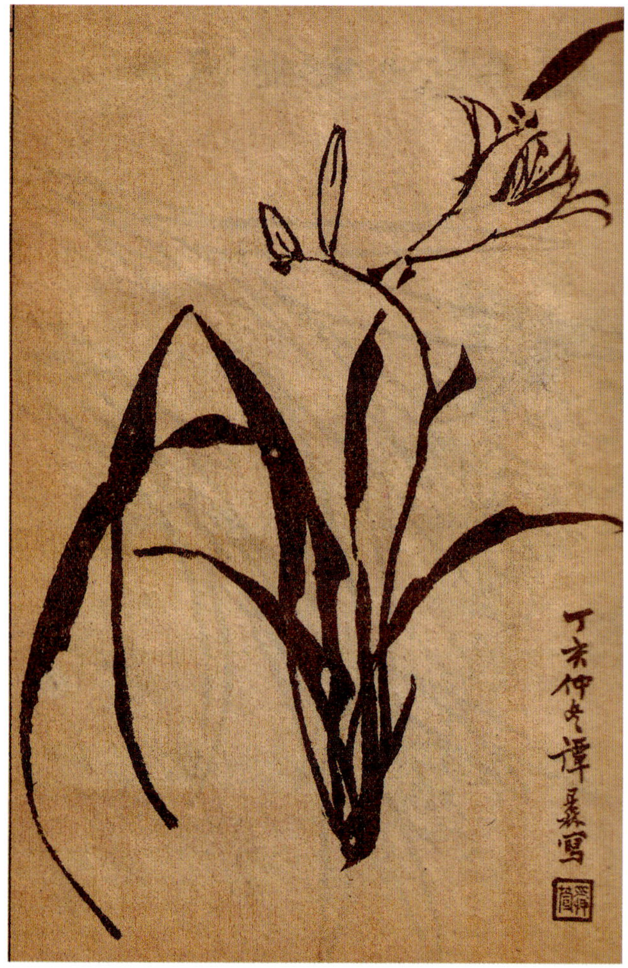

Chinese Day Lily (possibly Lan Cao)
from a reprint of the *Jiezi Yuan Hua Zhuan (Mustard Seed Garden Painting Manual)*, originally published in five voluems in 1679

Born in Xingshen county in today's Shandong province, Wang Dingguo (1048–after 1104) was the grandson of Wang Dan, Prime Minister during the reign of Shenzong (968–1022) of the Song dynasty. His given name was Wang Gong, his courtesy name Dingguo, and his pseudonym Qing Xusheng. He was a good friend of Su Shi (1037–1101), one of the best-known writers, calligraphers, painters, and poets of the Northern Song, who wrote a preface to a collection of Wang Dingguo's poetry. Wang was once exiled to Binzhou (a remote salt-producing town in the tropical south) for being implicated in a famous case against Su Shi, who was found guilty of writing seditious poetry. Wang was mentioned in "Biography of Wang Su" chapter of the *History of the Song* (*Song Shu*) as follows:

> Wang Gong is a talented person good at composing poems . . . Wang Gong was implicated in Su Shi's case and was exiled to Binzhou. He did not return until several years later and remained unyielding. Though having served in some important positions, he was removed from office several times due to his haughtiness.

Wang was a diligent scholar and his works include *Miscellanies, Random Notes in 1084*, *A Collection of Poems by Wang Dingguo*, *A Collection of Essays by Wang Dingguo*, and others. He was conscientious and principled, active in the political arena, and widely admired for his good character. In the preface to two of his own poems titled *Baibu Hong*, available in the collection *Three Hundred Song Poems*, (Shanghai: Ancient Book Press, 1989), Su Shi wrote:

> Wang Dingguo paid me a visit in Pengcheng [now Xuzhou in Jiangsu province]. One day, he went boating on the Sishui river with Yan Changdao and three singsong girls. They roamed north to Mount Shengnu and south to Baibuhong, having fun playing flutes and drinking wine, and did not return until the moon was high in the sky. Occupied with some personal matters, I did not join them in the journey. At night, in a feather robe, I stood at the Yellow Tower and watched them, thinking that the world had not had such a fun in the three hundred years since the death of Li Bai [701–762, a famous Tang poet]. After Dingguo had been gone for more than a month, I also boated to Baibuhong with Monk Senliao. Calling to mind the past, I could not help heaving a sigh. I wrote two poems, one for Senliao and the other for Dingguo.

Wang Dingguo was not only talented but had a variety of collections. Among his paintings was a work titled *Foggy River Surrounded by Rows of Mountains*, mentioned in a poem of Su Shi in 1088. The painting was the work of Wang Jinqing, the then emperor's son-in-law and a friend of Su Shi and Wang Dingguo.

Another story about Su Shi illuminates the attitudes of scholar-collectors of the day and their possessions: Su Shi had a Ying stone called *Qiuchi*, which happened to be coveted by Wang Jinqing, who asked Su to "lend" it to him. Knowing he would never get the stone back but finding it difficult to decline the request, Su Shi asked in return to "borrow" Wang Jinqing's *Grazing Horses* (*Muma Tu*), a work by Han Gan, a noted painter of the Tang dynasty. Since both scholars were reluctant to part with their treasures, Su thus retained his stone.

Wang Dingguo was also in close contact with Huang Tingjian (1045–1105), another famous poet, who mentioned Wang in one of his poems and wrote a preface to Wang's collection of essays. The fact that two great masters wrote poems and prefaces for Wang Dingguo shows that Wang was an extraordinary literary figure of the day, whose critical thinking is embodied in this essay.

In Praise of the Kunming Stone

Zhang Yanghao

A stone from the Southern Land is worth ten thousand taels of silver today. It had been washed by the water in the Kunming Pond of Chang'an and remained intact during the war-torn years. It matches the legendary luminous pearl in luster and the *lan cao* plant in its effectiveness in ensuring a male child. This remnant of the Kunming Pond dug during the Western Han can still be seen today, reminding people of the great accomplishments of Emperor Wu.

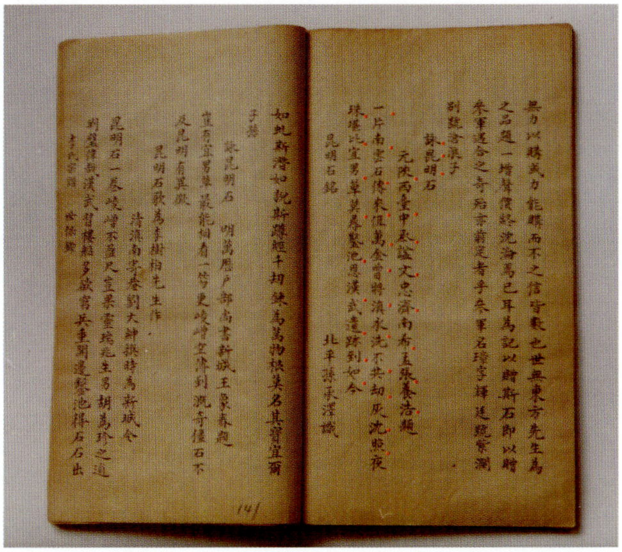

In Praise of the Kunming Stone
by Zhang Yanghao (1270–1329)
from the *Genealogy of the Li Family*

Zhang Yanghao (1270–1329), courtesy name Ximeng and pseudonym Wuqing, was born in Jinan, Shandong province. He was a high-ranking official of the Yuan dynasty, and once served as a public prosecutor but was demoted and lived in seclusion after his sharp criticism of the current politics offended those in power. During the reign of Tianli, the year 1329, the central region of Shaanxi province was hit by a serious drought. Zhang was sent there to provide relief for refugees and died from overwork while at the post.

Zhang was noted as composer of *sanqu*, a verse form popular in the Yuan dynasty; his works include *Yunzhuang Ballads* and *Yunzhuang Collection of Essays*, named after his residence Yunzhuang Villa. He was also a noted stone collector. Two famous Taihu garden stones, *Cangyun* (*Black Cloud*) and *Zhenyu* (*Inspired Jade*), were taken from Zhang's villa and are now in the Wang Yuyang Memorial Hall in Hengtai county, Shandong. On the back of the former is carved the name Zhang Yanghao and a *sanqu* composed by Zhang. Wang Yuyang (1634–1711) was a well-known Qing poet and a descendent of Wang Xiangchun and Wang Xiangqian.

Left: *Cangyun (Black Cloud);* right: *Zhenyu (Inspired Jade)*
Taihu gardens rocks once owned by Zhang Yanghao
Wang Yuyang Memorial Hall, Hengtai county, Shandong province
500 x 200 x 80 cm; 500 x 110 x 100 cm

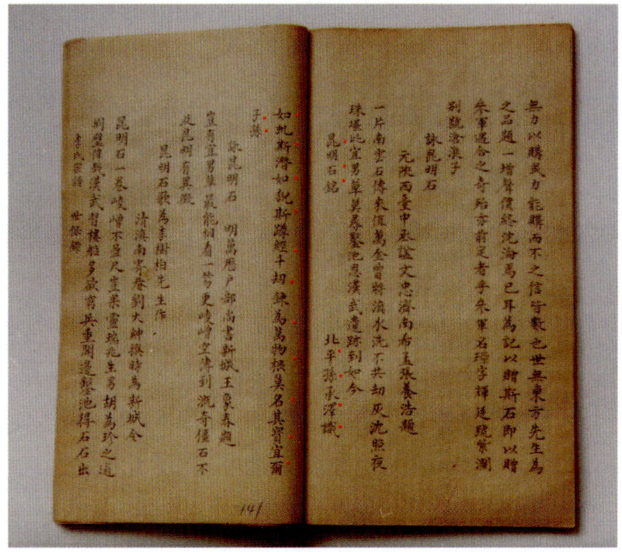

Epigraph on the Kunming Stone
Sun Chengze (fl 1627–44)
from the *Genealogy of the Li Family*

Epigraph on the Kunming Stone

Sun Chengze

> Swimming like a dragon and crouching like a wild beast, this spectacular stone has undergone thousands of misfortunes. As the root of all things, it is extremely precious, a blessing for the procreation of male offspring.

Sun Chengze, courtesy name Erbei and pseudonym Beihai, was born in Yidu, Shandong province. Sun was a *jin shi*, literally "presented scholar," a successful candidate in the highest imperial examination; during the reign of Emperor Chongzhen (1627–44), he served at the Ming imperial court. When the peasant Li Zicheng rebelled against Ming in 1644 to establish the short-lived Shun dynasty, Sun was responsible for the defense of Sichuan. Later he served as a historian in the following Qing dynasty. He had a wide variety of collections, and his works include *Geng Zi Xiao Geng Ji* and *Liu Shu Ji Jie*.

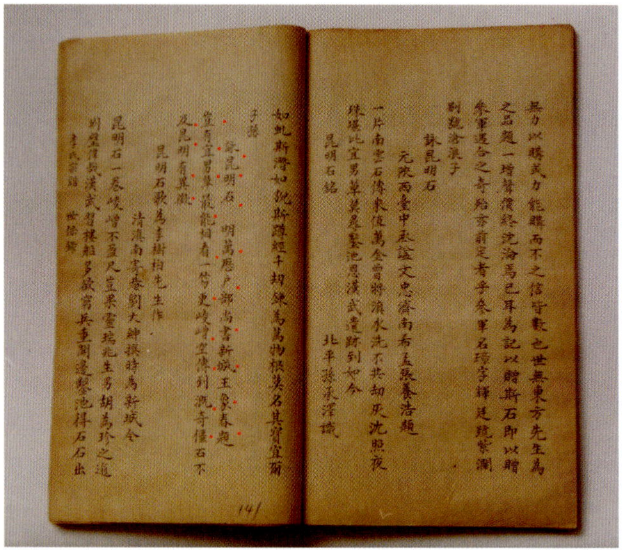

In Praise of the Kunming Stone
by Wang Xiangchun (1576–1631)
from the *Genealogy of the Li Family*

In Praise of the Kunming Stone

Wang Xiangchun

> Compared with the *lan cao* plant, this fantastic stone is even more effective in ensuring the birth of male children. Legend has it that even the well-known *Qijiang Stone* in the Liang dynasty cannot compare with this peculiar stone found in the Kunming Pond.

According to *Genealogy of the Wang Family*, Wang Xiangchun (1576–1631) was born in Xincheng county, today Hengtai county in Shandong province. His courtesy name was Jimu and his pseudonym Wenshui. He placed second in the imperial examination in 1610, during the reign of Emperor Wanli of the Ming dynasty (1368–1644). After serving as Imperial Examiner in Nanjing and later Minister of Finance, he was removed from office because his upright character offended some influential officials; he resumed his office during the second year of the Chongzheng era (1628). Wang was highly gifted and prolific. His works include four volumes of poems, titled *Wen Shan Ting*, and another volume titled *Qi Yin* (*Poems for Shandong*).

The *Qijiang Stone* he refers to was reputed to be a magnificent stone over sixteen feet tall. As is recorded in the *History of Southern Dynasty*, it was won by Emperor Wu (464–549) of the Liang dynasty (502–507) from his son in a game of *go.* The elder Wang died at age fifty-five in December of the fifth year of the Chongzheng reign (1631).

The Wang family was noted from the rein of Jiajing to that of Wanli of the Ming dynasty for the number of high-ranking officials it produced. The well-known art critic and calligrapher Dong Qichang (1634–1711) wrote on the memorial gateway of the Wang family four Chinese charac-

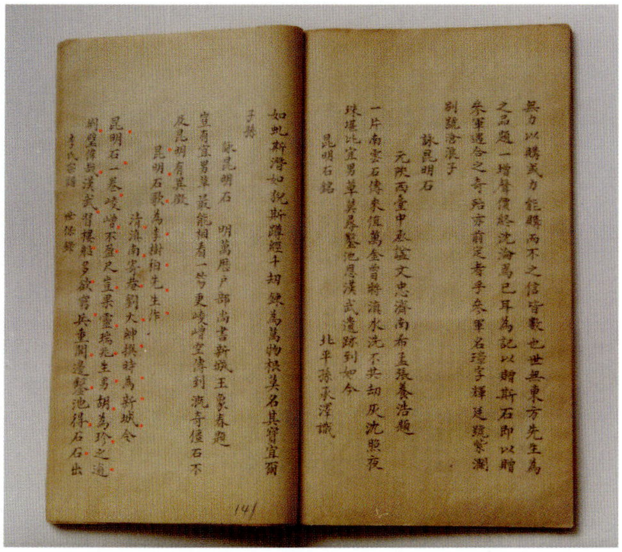

Song of the Kunming Stone
by Liu Dashen (1747–1828)
from the *Genealogy of the Li Family*

ters *Si shi guan bao*, meaning that four consecutive generations had served the imperial court. Recall that Wang Xiangqian (1546–1630), a peer of Wang Xiangchun, collected the two famous Taihu stones originally owned by Zhang Yanghao in the Yuan. Today there are still several other well-known Taihu garden stones in Shandong province collected by the Wang family.

Song of the Kunming Stone

Liu Dashen

This spectacular *Kunming Stone*, though
only about a foot in height, looks rigorous,
uncompromising, and weathered. Since
it promotes the birth of male offspring, it
has been cherished like jade. I recall that
Emperor Wu of the Western Han dynasty was
fond of naval warfare and actively engaged in
military ventures on the border. This spec-
tacular stone was found when digging the
Kunming Pond in Chang'an. Every time we
appreciate the stone, it reminds us of those
eventful times. You may ask where it comes
from, but how can a lifeless stone give you a
reply? Is it possible that it was transformed
from a stone unicorn to bless people with
more male offspring? Since ancient times,
most stone lovers have been peculiar in one
way or another and stones for them have only

served as elegant ornaments. Mi Fu addressed a stone as "older brother"; Su Dongpo, when praising his *Beihai* stone, told others that in his sleeves was hidden the vast Eastern Sea. Though both of them took stones to be their friends, it is still doubtful whether they had seen this *Kunming Stone*.

Li Shubai was a man of taste and fond of things ancient. He was in particular interested in such books as *Vast Records about Various Topics* [*Bowuzhi*, third century] and A Record of Current Stones [*Jinshilu*]. When he retired from office, he returned home accompanied only by this stone, but he seemed to be more broad-minded and impressive. His four sons were all brilliant and promising. Goodness, this peculiar stone has indeed worked miracles for his family! Most of the things in universe with longevity have no feelings, but this stone is really extraordinary. As I comment on this stone, the moonlight is shining on it through the window of the study.

According to *County Record of Hentai*, Shandong province, Liu Dashen (1747–1828), courtesy name Jiyan and pseudonym Tanxi, was born in Ningzhou, Yunnan province. He was *jin shi*, passing the highest imperial examination in during the rein of Emperor Qianlong and served as the magistrate of Xincheng county from 1783 to 1787. He was fond of poetry and left a collection of his own verse for posterity. His testimonial above was written after Li Shubai brought this stone from Shanxi Province. In it he repeats the story of the excavation of the Kunming Pond to practice naval warfare tactics. The mythical animal he refers to, the *qilin*, resembled a winged unicorn; sightings of it were considered auspicious omens.

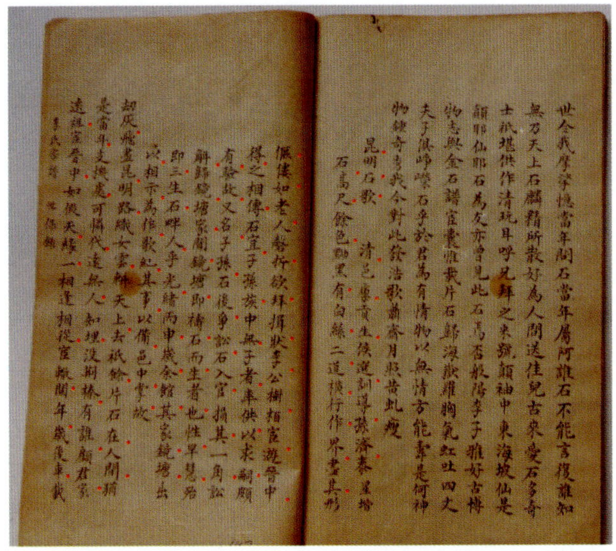

In Praise of the Kunming Stone
by Sun Jitai (fl (1825–1908)
from the *Genealogy of the Li Family*

In Praise of the Kunming Stone

Sun Jitai

The peculiar stone is about one foot in height, dark and dusky, with two white veins on it. It resembles an old man bending his back, as if bowing down. Li Shubai bought it when he was an official in Shanxi province. Legend has it that this stone will bless pregnant women to give birth to male children. Therefore, members of the Li family without a son all worshipped it and finally their wishes were fulfilled. Later, the Li family was involved in a lawsuit and the stone seized by the government; in this process one of its corners was slightly damaged. After the case was over, the stone was placed in the hands of Li Jingtang. It was said that Li's parents once worshipped the stone and finally gave birth to him, who was exceptionally intelligent and gifted. In 1896, when I was tutoring in Li Jingtang's home, he showed me the stone and I wrote an essay to record what had happened with it as an anecdote.

The Kunming Pond is today nowhere to be found, and gone with it are the Herd Boy and Weaving Girl stones placed on its bank by Emperor Wu of the Western Han. What remains is only this wonderful stone, like that used by the legendary Weaving Girl to support her loom. All these anecdotes are unknown to most people today due to the passage of time. It is said that the ancestor of Li Jingtang, then an official in Shanxi province, had the luck to acquire this stone, which accompanied him for many years before being brought to Shandong province upon his retirement from office. Having heard that worshipping the stone would promote male offspring, the Li family took the stone as its heirloom and every succeeding household took turns offering incense to it, seldom considering the good deeds needed to accumulate merit for succeeding generations and consequently resulting in constant family discord. As it is always the case, heirlooms are destined to suffer from misfortunes and it is only natural they had such experience. After all these unpleasant happenings, the stone brought auspiciousness to the Li family again. Though it is still heart-stirring to hear about such anecdotes as the giant stone fish in the Kunming Pond flapping its scales in a thunderstorm and someone becoming pregnant after dreaming about a jade swallow flying into her body, this stone is even more amazing. There is no need to admire others' possession of gold and silver, as this stone itself is an invaluable asset. Yesterday the Li family showed me the stone, which looked grayish and conveyed a sense of antiquity. I hope that the Li's will protect the stone well, value the moral virtues handed down from their ancestors, and maintain their fine family tradition.

Sun Jitai, courtesy name Xingjie and pseudonym Tieqiao, was a scholar during the rein of Emperor Guangxu (1825–1908) of the Qing dynasty. According to *County Record of Zichuan* in Shandong province, Sun Jitai was selected to study in Guozi Jian, the highest institution of learning at that time. His family had a long tradition of learning and growing up he studied with his elder brother Sun Jikui. Together, they appreciated excellent writing and debated controversial points, teaching and encouraging each other. Sun Jitai was good at composing classic Chinese prose. During the Nian Rebellion (an armed uprising in northern China from 1853 to 1868), he and his family fled their hometown, but even in the turmoil and chaos of war, he continued to study. When his elder brother served as the supervisor of Zouxian county, he lectured in Lüping Academy of Classical Learning. Every time he visited his brother, he would help write critiques of examination papers. People who saw his comments were all amazed and admired his talent. He stayed at home and looked after his father Sun Dongquan, who lived nearly to be nearly ninety years old. Not until the death of his father and the completion of the mourning did he take part in the imperial examination and successfully pass at the county level. He was granted with a food subsidy by the government and began to teach. Many of his students were famous intellectuals at that time. His work includes *A Collection of the Poems and Essays by Tieqiao*. Li Jintang, who took possession of the stone after the lawsuit described, was of the eleventh generation of the Li family.

Conclusions

The purpose of this essay is to investigate the likelihood that the *Kunming Stone* we know today actually dates from the Han dynasty. Nearly 1200 years elapsed from its unearthing in 120 BCE to Wang Dingguo's encounter with it in the home of Administrator Xu in 1057. Another 950 years passed before I was privileged to examine it at the home of Mr. Sun in Zibo City. How likely is it that I saw there the stone of history and legend dating from the Western Han, a stone in the possession of owners known and unknown, famous and perhaps infamous, for nearly two millennium? Although we may never be able to answer this question with absolute certainly, when we consider key aspects of Chinese history and culture, we find no compelling reason to doubt this is the case. Let us consider especially Chinese early philosophy and folk beliefs, including attitudes about stones and nature, reverence for antiquity, and a penchant for documentation not only of history and genealogy but also of anecdotes about the mysterious and supernatural.

Although appreciation of what are today regarded as scholars' rocks has a documented history dating back to the Tang dynasty, Chinese reverence for stones as embodying the elemental natural force of *qi* dates to prehistory. From legends like that of the goddess Nü Wa, who patched up the heavens with a mixture smelted from stones of five colors, we know that Chinese have revered the power of stones since time immemorial. The earliest Chinese historical text, the *Shu Jing* (*Book of History*, third century BCE) notes that stones were presented as tribute to Yu the Great, the tamer of floods and legendary founder of China's first dynasty, the Xia. Stones with ponds and islands in imperial parks like the Shanglin represented in human scale both the empire and the distant mountain ranges beyond, including abodes of the immortals like Kunlun to the west and Penglai to the east. Han dynasty stone legends include those of the Herd Boy and Weaving Girl stones placed on the bank of the Kunming Pond, and a fish-shaped stone that flapped its scales and tail during thunderstorms. As well, there is a legend of Qianying stone from the sea of Anhai. Purportedly blue in color and light as a feather, it remains warm in the coldest winter, while becoming cool in the heat of summer. When carved into the shape of a person, it morphs into an exact likeness. Emperor Wu had this stone carved into an image of Lady Li, his favorite concubine who had passed away. When placed behind silk curtains, the statue looked exactly like his beloved consort at her most beautiful.

In traditional Chinese society male children were favored over female. For the upper classes, sons were needed to pass the state examinations, win posts in government, and so add to the family fortune and reputation; among the peasantry of an agriculture-based society, sons were needed to work in the fields. Daughters could be an expensive luxury, requiring dowries to attract husbands. A stone that could facilitate the birth of male children would be miraculous indeed, and a far more compelling reason than aesthetic considerations to preserve it over many generations. The value placed on the *Kunming Stone* is evident in testimonials to it: "The stone passed down has the worth of ten thousand taels of silver" and "There is no need to admire the gold and silver possessed by others, as this stone itself is an invaluable asset." That the stone's worth was widely acknowledged is further indicated by Sun Jitai's report of it being confiscated by the government due to a law-

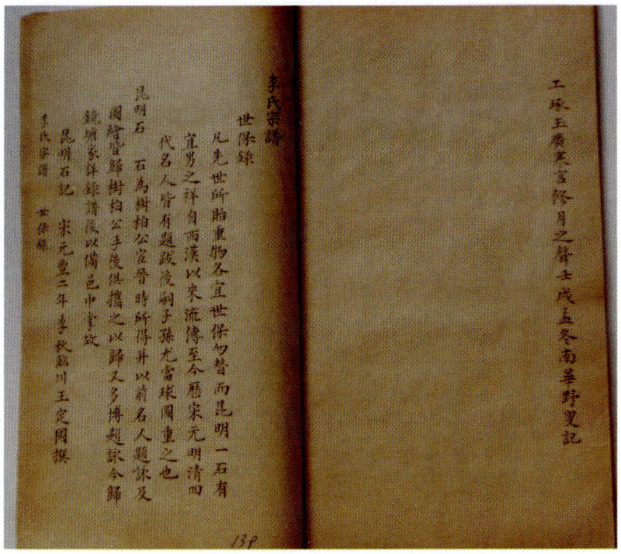

Exhortation to Li family descendants
to safeguard the *Kunming Stone,*
from the *Li Family Genealogy*

suit. Its purported power to bless pregnant women with male offspring made it highly valuable, and is the main reason for it being safeguarded and handed down over the generations.

Throughout Chinese history illustrious clans have kept genealogies to record for posterity important figures, events, and accomplishments. The *Genealogy of the Li Family* now consists of five volumes, containing records of births and deaths, stories of virtuous and meritorious conduct, literary and military accompaniments, government postings, honors received, records of gardens and collections, and other anecdotes. Information about the *Kunming Stone* is recorded in the third volume, which states that it was purchased by Li Shubo, of the seventh generation of the Li family, who served as a county magistrate in Shanxi province during the Qianlong reign (1736–95). The *County Record of Zichuan* confirms that Li Shubo was the courtesy name of Li Hui, whose pseudonym was Yangsheng. He was originally a clerk in Yangcheng county of Shanxi province and was promoted several times to become the magistrate of Changzi county. According to the *Genealogy*, at the time he purchased the stone, he also acquired paintings, poems, and inscriptions in praise of it composed by notables of previous dynasties. When the stone was later brought to Shandong province, more poems and inscriptions in praise of it were written. However, none of these are extant, only those copied into the *Genealogy*. Such documents might easily be lost or, considering most were written by illustrious scholars and calligraphers, possibly sold or even stolen.

Nevertheless, the *Kunming Stone* was kept in the Li family for nearly 250 years, over eight generations, which is a remarkable accomplishment. It is said that the Li family buried the stone during the turmoil of the Cultural Revolution (1966–76), when antiquities were being deliberately destroyed, and as a result, the original wooden base for it was lost. The documented actions of both the Xu and Li families demonstrate that along with other family treasures illustrious Chinese families have actively engaged in the acquisition and protection of important stones.

Consequently, the fact that this stone has been the subject of poems and inscriptions from the Song dynasty is not as remarkable as it might seem. The earliest record of the most well-known ancient stone, the *Baojin Studio Yanshan*, dates from the rein of Emperor Li Yu (937–978) of the Southern Tang dynasty. Poems and essays in praise of the *Shuangshi* (*Twin Peaks*) stone owned by Bai Juyi in the Tang and the *Qiuchi* stone owned by Su Shi in the Song also remain. Regrettably, however, the stones themselves are all lost. Still, such records show that composing poems and essays for beloved stones, as for other treasured possessions, was a common practice of Chinese connoisseurs. The fact that so many noted scholars throughout a number of dynasties composed testimonials for the *Kunming Stone*, indicates not only acknowledgment of its value and its impressive historical connections, but also that its owners were equal in rank and fame with the celebrity composers, patriarchs of families such as the Xu and the Li. From what they wrote, it is clear that these discerning scholars were convinced that the stone they were viewing was indeed the female stone taken from the Kunming Pond. As Zhang Yanghao asserted in the Yuan dynasty: "This remnant of the Kunming Pond dug during the Western Han can still be seen today, reminding people of the great accomplishments of Emperor Wu."

Finally, we must consider the description of the stone from several passages in the *Geneology*, where it is likened to "a dragon holding its head high and swimming underwater or like a predator crouching on the ground." It is further described as about one foot in height, "dark in color, with two white veins, resembling a bent old man." These words precisely describe the present stone.

This study of the *Kunming Stone* is not only to acknowledge recognition due to the stone itself but more importantly to mark a major discovery in Chinese stone appreciation history. Current documentation of stone appreciation by Chinese men of letters dates back a thousand years, to the late Tang dynasty; however the *Kunming Stone* was purportedly collected over two thousand years ago. Though the precise events cannot be confirmed today, from the mere fact that the stories were transmitted we can infer that people in the Han appreciated and even worshipped stones, whether for different or similar reasons that those of the Tang. Believing a stone can induce male

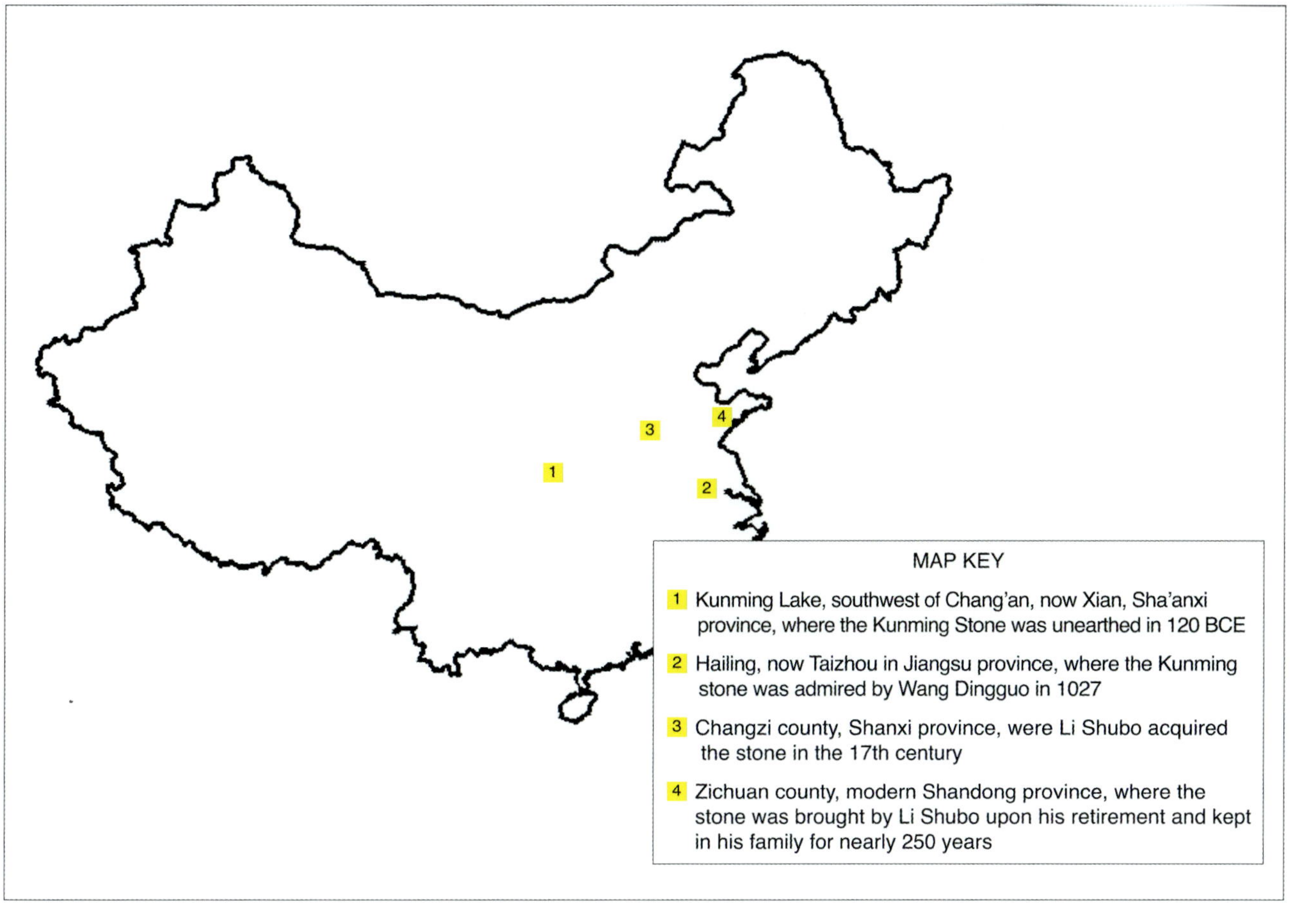

offspring is no more or less an imaginative leap than regarding it as representing it as the abode of immortals. Both conform to the beliefs of the people of their day, and both are rooted in assumptions of a fundamental affinity between man and nature.

In the third volume of the *Geneology of the Li Family* it is recorded (see p. 111): "Efforts should be made to protect important objects left from ancient times and to hand them down to later generations. As the *Kunming Stone* is auspicious for its power to facilitate male offspring, it has been passed down from the Western Han dynasty to today, with inscriptions and poems of notables of the Song, Yuan, Ming, and Qing dynasties. Our descendants should therefore treasure it."

It appears that for over two millennia every plausible effort has been made to live up to the spirit of this directive. We must therefore extend our thanks to the stone connoisseurs of many dynasties, without whom we would not have the opportunity to marvel at this wonderful object today. As well we must thank the many scholars who left us with testimonials and descriptions of the *Kunming Stone*, evidence of its identity as a relic of the Han. Although in the end, belief is in the mind of the beholder, it is wise to recall what Wang Dingguo wrote: "The universe, as we can see, is vast and everything in it so changeable. There is indeed nothing that is impossible. Those who believe only what they see or hear and deny the existence of what they cannot see or hear are short-sighted, and underestimate the power of nature."

Fei Niao (Flying Bird)
Lingbi stone, Lingbi county, Anhui province
44 x 35 x 14 cm, 20th c wooden stand

Selected Ancient Writings on Stones

From the preface to the Ti'an Shipu (Ti'an Stone Catalogue)

by Zhu Jiuding

Known as the "Ti'an Hermit," Zhu Jiuding was a writer in the late Ming and early Qing dynasties. His deep passion for stones led to his reputation as a "stone fanatic."

Many ancient scholars, such as Mi Fu and Su Shi, were fond of stones and have been continually admired for their refined taste. Quite a number of my friends also love stones. Ji Bozi, whose sobriquet was "Unrestrained Old Man of Mount Zhong," brought me two stones when he returned from Fujian. One of them was known as *Qiu Shan* [*Autumn Mountain*] and the other *Mu Shan* [*Evening Mountain*]. I was so fond of them that I could hardly tear myself away from them.

Zhang Youliang, styled Zhang Qizhang, from Zouping paid a visit to Hangzhou and in his sleeve was hidden a stone of no more than one *cun* [about 3.3 cm] high, whose shape closely resembled that of a bamboo root. Fascinated, I composed a poem for it. Youliang was so enamored of stones that he once used three hundred oxen to drag a huge, well-shaped yellow stone back to his rear garden after discovering it during a tour of Mount Changbai. He often told others that this stone closely resembled the grotesque stones in Mi Fu's paintings.

Yao Bofu of Guandong was also a stone fanatic. Every time I paid him a visit, he would show me the fine stones he had collected, displaying them on a table. Some of these stones included Lingyan stones from Yunnan and Sichuan, and Chu stones from Yongkang of Zhejiang. Moreover, in his collection, there was a stone tortoise, which he treasured highly and "raised" in a Han-dynasty copper vessel. It was always his stones that delayed me for a whole day every time I visited him.

When I was a child, I once followed my father to the Fishing Terrace of Yan Ziling, who was a well-known hermit of the Eastern Han dynasty, at the foot of Mount Fuchun. There I searched far and wide for fine stones on the sandy beach until my shoes were virtually worn out. How ridiculous is this mania for stones! Now, when I have the chance to travel to Sichuan, I cannot help but recall these lines from Du Fu's poetry: "The roads in Sichuan are lined on both sides with grasses and flowers; and the river beaches there abound in fine stones." I asked my attendant to look for stones along the riversides and he came back with a dozen of them, all exquisite and unusual.

Later, I obtained several more strange stones at Zhenwu Pond in Zhongjiang county. I then wrote a catalogue for all the stones I had collected, describing their shapes and singing their praises. I plan to ask Xian Yao and Xie Bin to compile a catalogue with pictures of these stones and show both stones and catalogue to Bozhi, Youliang, and Bofu, because on the one hand we share the same interest in stones and on the other I feel that what I did with the stones might live up to the expectations of the ancients.

—Zhu Jiuding, native of Qiantang known as the Hermit of Ti'an, composed this at the side of the Zhiji stone in Junping

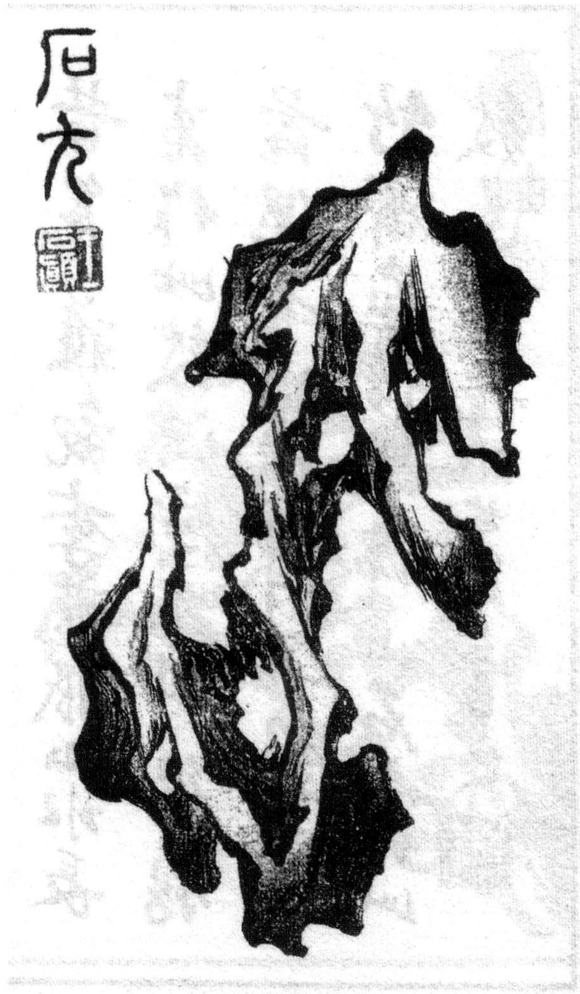

One of the *Sixty-five Stones of the Xuanhe Period* painted by Wang Yemei, from a reprint of the *Yemei Shipu (Yemei Stone Catalogue),* originally published before 1692

From the preface of the Yemei Shipu (Yemei Stone Catalogue)

by Wang Yemei

Also known as Wang Yin, Wang Yemei was a painter during the Qing dynasty. Born in Nanjing, he once visited Osaka, Japan. To create the *Yemei Stone Catalogue*, he painted the *Sixty-five Stones of the Xuanhe Period* of the Northern Song dynasty (1119–1125) and furnished each with a poem; the catalogue was published no later than 1692.

> Since childhood, I had formed the habit of "reading books without understanding them deeply." I developed deep affection for Tang poetry and Jin calligraphy and had a great passion for the six painting techniques passed down from the Southern Qi dynasty. I admired most Mi Fu and his son Mi Youren of the Song dynasty, and five of the major painters—Gao Fangshan, Wang Meng, Huang Gongwang, Wuzhen, and Ni Zan—of the Yuan dynasty and could hardly tear myself away from their works. I copied their painting as models untiringly from early in the morning until late at night, almost forgetting to eat and sleep. As a result, I obtained some basic painting skills, which in turn fueled my enthusiasm in painting.
>
> I was thus infatuated with painting. For the next thirty years and more I suffered a great deal from this interest and at the same time enjoyed it enormously, though I achieved nothing significant in the field. It was true that I liked painting mountains, water, people, flowers, fish, and worms, but stones remained my favorite [subject]. Every time I saw a fine stone, it seemed to me very congenial, although maybe it was I who loved stones, not vice versa. Therefore, I named myself Shidian [Stone Fanatic] and my study Aishi [Loving Stones]. On my tables were placed grotesque stones and in my courtyard were installed supernatural stones, so that I could enjoy and appreciate them during the

breaks of my study. Whenever I was told the whereabouts of a fine stone I would go and enjoy it to my heart's content and would paint a picture of it in an instant. In fact, I spent much of my time discussing stones with scholar-bureaucrats, inquiring about fine stones, painting pictures of them and singing their praises, finding great delight in searching for and appreciating magnificent stones.

I fell in love with stones as if by fate. I once had the chance to peruse the *Suyuan Stone Catalogue* and was fascinated by the pictures of the *Sixty-five Xuanhe Stones* in it. Delighted, I started to paint the stones and furnished each with a poem. Every time I opened the album, I felt as if those sixty-five stones were right before my eyes. As my friends also loved this collection, I had it printed and shared it with others with a similar interest. Since I am clumsy of hand, I may not have embodied the spirit of these stones in my paintings, though they might look fine in shape. It is up to viewers to decide whether the paintings are worthy or not.

Three of the *Sixty-five Stones of the Xuanhe Period* painted by Wang Yemei, from a reprint of the *Yemei Shipu (Yemei Stone Catalogue),* originally published before 1692

From the Jiezi Yuan Hua Zhuan (Mustard Seed Garden Painting Manual)

published by Li Yu

This well-known manual of Chinese painting was compiled during the early Qing dynasty by Shen Xinyou. Shen was the son-in-law of the famous playwright Li Yu (1611–1679), whose mansion in Jinling was known as Jiezi Yuan, or Mustard Seed Garden. To produce a manual for landscape painting, Shen commissioned the editing of the teaching materials of Li Liufang, a painter of the late Ming. The first of the manual's five volumes, with a preface by Li Yu, was published in 1679.

> *Zhou* [interior brush texturing] is a technique commonly used in traditional landscape painting. It includes a large variety of techniques, such as *pima zhou* [hemp-fiber texture stroke], *luanma zhou* [tangled hemp strokes],

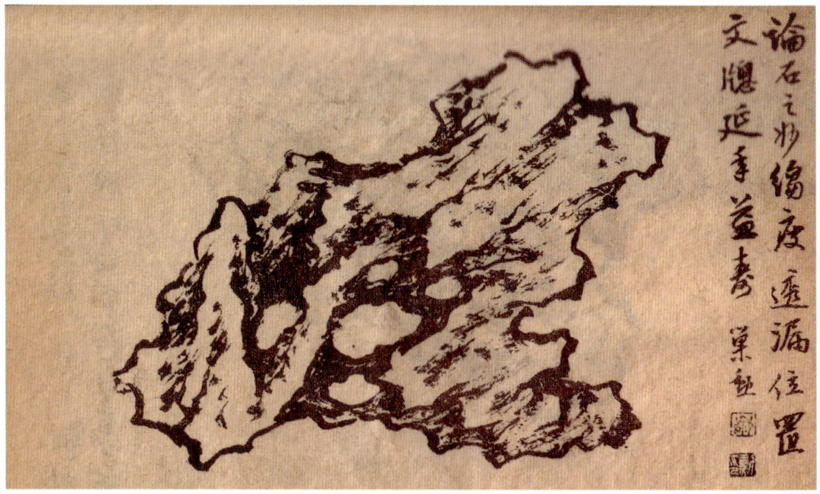

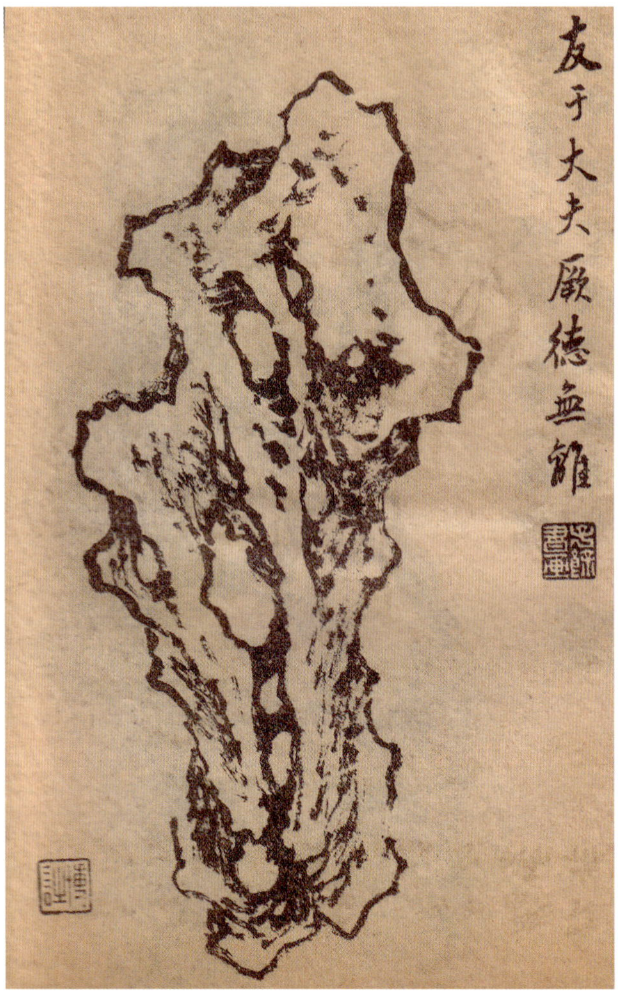

Two stone paintings from a reprint of *JieziYuan Hua Zhuan (Mustard Seed Garden Painting Manual)* originally published in five volumes in 1679

zhima zhou [sesame strokes], *dafu zhou* [big axe-cut strokes], *yuntou zhou* [cloud head strokes], *liangdian zhou* [two-dot strokes], *heye zhou* [lotus leaf strokes], *fantou zhou* [alum-head stroke], *gulou zhou* [human-skeleton strokes], *guipi zhou* [ghost-face strokes], *jiesuo zhou* [raveled-rope strokes], *luanchai zhou* [disordered firewood strokes], *niumao zhou* [ox-hair strokes], *maya zhou* [horse-tooth strokes], and so on. In accordance with different methods of representation, combinations of other texture strokes are also employed to enhance the effects of paintings.

At first, a three-dimensional painting technique was employed for painting stones. When we observe a person, we note his or her impressive manners and moral integrity; similarly, when we paint a stone, we focus on the vitality it possesses, since it is a "bone" of heaven and earth as reflected in the nickname "root of clouds." Just as a bone without vitality is rotten, so a stone possessed of no

vitality is insensate. How can rotten bones and insensate stones appear in the works of scholars? Therefore, no effort should be made to paint such stones. However, even if a stone does possess an imposing manner, it is extremely difficult to capture its vitality in a painting, since this is so subtle and elusive. Therefore, it is unwise to start to paint stones before one has a ready plan in mind and a superb command of the painting skills. For me, painting stones is not all that difficult since I have grasped the relevant painting techniques.

A stone is three-dimensional, possessing surface irregularities, a height and thickness, edges and corners, and shapes of mountains and rivers, which work together to create its vitality. Only when one is familiar with all these elements in a stone can one grasp its real pre-eminence. In fact, there is nothing mysterious about painting stones and all can be summarized in one word: versatility.

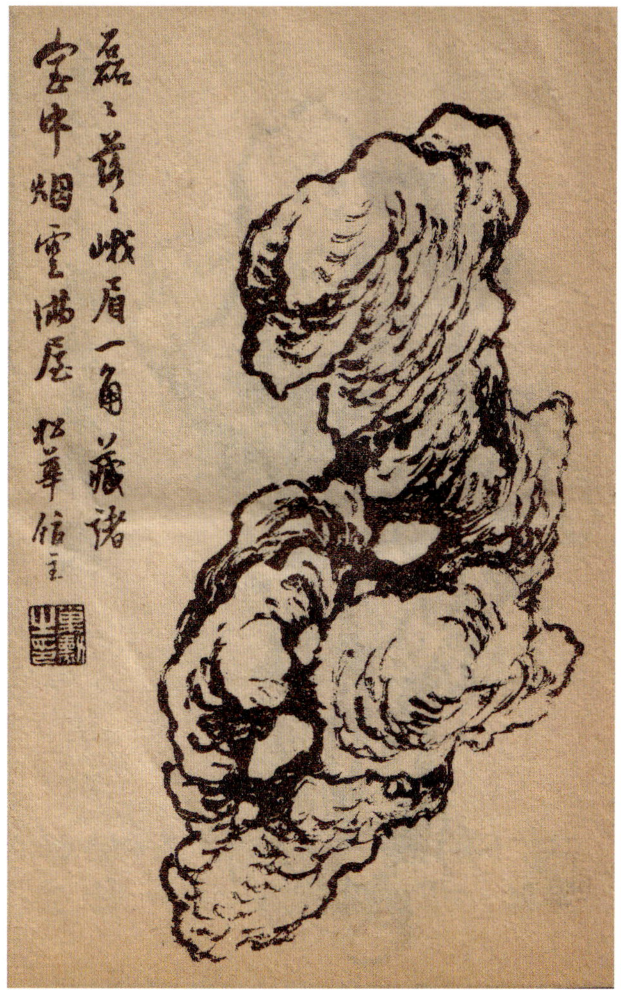

Two stone paintings from a reprint of *JieziYuan Hua Zhuan (Mustard Seed Garden Painting Manual)* originally published in five volumes in 1679

Meihua Lu (Sika Deer)
Carved pearl Lingbi stone, Lingbi county, Anhui province
25 x 18 x 10 cm, 19th c boxwood stand

Stone-like and Related Objects

Chinese philosophy assumes affinities between all the "myriad things" of the natural and human worlds, and Chinese intellectuals have always observed and appreciated these connections. From examples in previous chapters, we know that object and representation is a two-way street. Stones may be appreciated for their resemblance to other natural objects, not only mountains, caves, and streams, but also various animals and figures; likewise objects made of other natural or crafted materials may be seen to represent stones, and by extension mountains and landscape elements. Stones may look like birds or animals; wood or glass may look like majestic peaks.

Thus over the centuries collecting interests have broadened to include artifacts exhibiting the form or spirit of natural stones but made from a variety of other materials. We have seen some ceramic examples already, notably an ink stone with twelve peaks from the Han dynasty (see p. 32) and the *Elegant and Magnificent Peak* and others (beginning p. 84). With the increased wealth and improved material technologies of later dynasties, notably the Qing (1644–1911) came a wider variety of stone-like creations. Recall that the Qianlong Emperor, who ruled from 1736 to 1796, was one of three great imperial connoisseurs of stones, and many examples of his collecting activities can be seen in the Palace Museums of both Beijing and Taipei.

Examples here include stones resembling deer, horses, waves, even a hand of the Buddha. Of particular interest are so-called chrysanthemum stones, with crystalline formations resembling those prized flowers, and used often to fashion the ink stones that were one of the "four treasures" of the scholars' studio. Also shown are stone-like objects fashioned from metal, glass, or porcelain, or carved from wood, root, jade, and even from stone, especially the colorful Shoushan stone traditionally used to make seals. As well there are natural formations of deer horn, coral, and tree root. Although the forms and materials may appear disparate and unrelated, all resonate in the mind of the true stone lover with the exuberant spirit of "respected stones," *gongshi*.

Kongzi Feng (Confucius Peak)
Stone type unknown
52 x 28 x 17 cm, 18th c wooden stand

Laozi Feng (Laozi Peak)
Stone type unknown
40 x 16 x 12 cm, 19th c wooden stand

Opposite: *Tian Ma Xing Kong (Heavenly Horse Galloping Skyward)*
Lingbi stone, Lingbi county, Anhui province
12 x 12 x 4 cm, one stone with six 20th c wooden stands

Inkstone
Chrysanthemum stone, Liuyang county, Hunan province
22 x 15 x 4 cm

Two inkstones
Chrysanthemum stone, Liuyang county, Hunan province
21 x 15 x 3 cm (left) and 21 x 15 x 6 cm (right)

Brush pot, inkstone, water containers
Chrysanthemum stone, Liuyang county, Hunan province, modern stands

Qian Nian Hua (Eternal Flowers)
Chrysanthemum stone, Liuyang county, Hunan province
28 x 29 x 11 cm, 18th c wooden stand

Below: *Vase*
Carved Boshan Wen stone, Shandong province
28 x 21 x 19 cm, 18th to 19th c wooden stand

Above: *Owl*
Carved stone, type unknown
26 x 11 x 8 cm, 19th c wooden stand

Above: *Stone chime*
Lingbi stone, Lingbi county, Anhui province
5 x 11 x 1 cm, 20th c wooden stand

Ling Xiu Taihu (Delicate Taihu Stones)
Pair of carved stones, type unknown
33 x 14 x 40 cm, 20th c wooden stands

Above: *Xue Lang Shi (Snow Wave Stone)*
Stone type unknown
18 x 23 x 10 cm, 18th to 19th c wooden stand

Left: *Xiong Di Tong Gen (Brotherhood Root)*
Fossilized deer horn
24 x 22 x 6 cm, 20th c wooden stand

Opposite: *Wu Lao Qi Feng (Five Old Men Peak)*
Shoushan stone
45 x 22x 13 cm, 18 to 19th c wooden stand
An inscription on the back translates: "This Five Old Men Peak [is presented to wish] Fenyang prosperity and longevity," with a seal that reads: "Collected and preserved by Meng Shu Cun."

Miao Qu Tian Cheng (Natural Wit and Humor)
Shoushan stone, title inscribed by Wang Chong (1494–1533)
10 x 14 x 6 cm, 20th c wooden stand

Mo Yu Tong Ling (Divine Black Jade)
Soapstone scholars' stone
21 x 22 x 5 cm, 20th c wooden stand

Mu Zi Qing Shen (Motherly Love)
Soapstone scholars' stone
22 x 15 x 8 cm, 18th to 19th c wooden stand

Taihu Stone
Tricolor ceramic scholars' stone 19th c
21 x 19 x 6 cm, 20th c wooden stand

Jin Shan Sheng Hui (Splendid Golden Cliffs)
Liuli glass scholars' stone
13 x 24 x 6 cm, 20th c wooden stand

Above: *Jing Lang (Contending Waves)*
Liuli glass scholars' stone
13 x 24 x 6 cm, 20th c wooden stand

Below: *Lu Lang Yong Dong (Green Surge)*
Liuli glass scholars' stone
40 x 32 x 14 cm, 20th c wooden stand

Bu Bu Gao Sheng (Ascending the Heights)
Jade scholars' stone
20 x 30 x 14 cm, 20th c wooden stand

Chun Lu Qingcheng Shan (Spring Green over Qingcheng Mountain)
Jadeite-like scholars' stone
28 x 18 x 18 cm, 18th c wooden stand

Above: *Shu Zhan (Unfolding)*
Pink coral
31 x 35 x 19 cm, 19th c wooden stand

Opposite: *Gui Fei Zui Jiu (Drunken Concubine)*
Wooden coral
43 x 20 x 14 cm, 18th c wooden stand

Wu Ban 2 (Dancing Partner 2)
Metal scholars' stone
35 x 16 x 16 cm, 20th c wooden stand

Opposite: *Wu Ban 1 (Dancing Partner 1)*
Metal scholars' stone
34 x 18 x 9 cm, 18th to 19th c wooden stand

Left: Guo Shi Lei Lei (Heaps of Fruit)
Copper scholars' stone
34 x 11 x 7 cm, 19th c wooden stand

XuanYan (Sheer Precipice)
Cast copper scholars' stone
21 x 45 x 21 cm

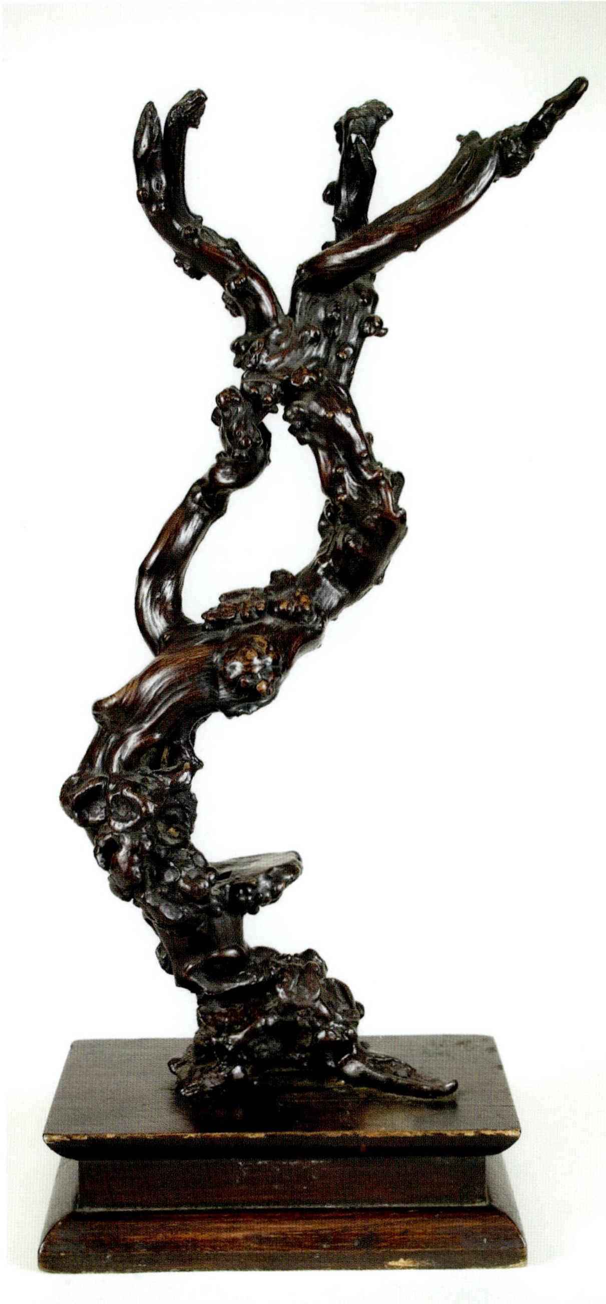

Above: *A Na Duo Zi (Willowy Beauty)*
Tree root scholars' stone
62 x 25 x 16 cm, 17th to 18th c wooden stand

Ba Xiu (Surpassing Delicate)
Wumo (ebony wood) scholars' stone
59 x 8 x 4 cm, 19th c wooden stand

Peach Tree
Carved *zitan* wood, 19th c
15 x 7 x 5 cm, 19th c wooden stand

Opposite: *Vase*
Carved bamboo root, 18th c
26 x 14 x 8 cm, 18th c wooden stand

Brush rest
Carved *zitan* wood, 19th c
9 x 15 x 6 cm, 19th c two-layer stand, of *zitan* and boxwood

Right: *Zi Zai (Being There)*
Tree root scholars' stone, 18th to 19th c
22 x 11 x 9 cm, 18th to 19th c wooden stand

Brush pot
Tree root, 19th c
30 x 24 x 22 cm, 19th c wooden stand

Above: *Fu Shou (Buddha's Hand)*
Laoshan green stone, Shandong province
19 x 8 x 6 cm, 19th c wooden stand

Shang Cheng Feng Mao (Village on a Bluff)
Carved wooden scholars' stone, 17th c or earlier
44 x 20 x 10 cm, 17th c or earlier wooden stand

A group of small scholars' stones
Stand 77 x 50 x 8 cm

A group of small metal scholars' stones
Stand 77 x 50 x 8 cm

A group of small scholars' stones
Stand 47 x 37 x 8 cm

Chinese Characters for Stone Titles

Floating World Editions publishes books that contribute to a deeper understanding of Asian cultures. Editorial supervision: Ray Furse. Book and cover design: Liz Trovato. Production supervision: Bill Rose. Printing and binding: SNP LeeFung, China. The typefaces used are Perpetua and Trajan.